Introduction to Networking Lab Manual

Dr. Theodor Richardson

PEARSON IT CERTIFICATION

800 East 96th Street

Indianapolis, Indiana 46240 USA

Introduction to Networking Lab Manual

ISBN-13: 978-0-13-309638-5

ISBN-10: 0-13-309638-6

Library of Congress Cataloging-in-Publication data is on file.

Printed in the United States of America

First Printing: September 2012

Trademarks

Warning and Disclaimer

Bulk Sales

Pearson IT Certification offers excellent discounts on this book when ordered in quantity for bulk purchases or special sales. For more information, please contact

> **U.S. Corporate and Government Sales**
>
> **1-800-382-3419**
>
> **corpsales@pearsontechgroup.com**

For sales outside of the U.S., please contact

> **International Sales**
>
> **international@pearsoned.com**

Associate Publisher
Dave Dusthimer

Executive Editor
Brett Bartow

Senior Development Editor
Christopher Cleveland

Managing Editor
Sandra Schroeder

Senior Project Editor
Tonya Simpson

Copy Editor
John Edwards

Proofreader
Debbie Williams

Technical Editor
Sean Wilkins

Publishing Coordinator
Vanessa Evans

Book Designer
Mark Shirar

Compositor
Studio Galou

Contents at a Glance

Introduction   xiv

CHAPTER 1   Introduction to Computer Data   2

CHAPTER 2   Introduction to Computer Networking   34

CHAPTER 3   Building TCP/IP Networks   58

CHAPTER 4   Transmitting Bits   76

CHAPTER 5   Ethernet LANs   96

CHAPTER 6   Wireless LANs   114

CHAPTER 7   Wide-Area Networks   134

CHAPTER 8   The Internet Protocol (IP)   148

CHAPTER 9   The Internet   162

CHAPTER 10 TCP/IP Transport   176

Table of Contents

Introduction   xiv

Chapter 1   **Introduction to Computer Data**   2

Lab 1.1: Reading Binary   2

Breaking Down Decimal Values   3

Mapping Binary Values   3

Binary Conversion   4

Decimal Conversion   6

Creating a Conversion Worksheet   7

Lab 1.1 Review   11

Lab 1.2: Binary Math and Logic   11

Binary Addition   11

AND/OR Logic   12

Binary Operations Practice   14

Lab 1.2 Review   14

Lab 1.3: Bit and Byte Structure   15

Byte Construction   15

Byte Storage Capacity   16

Hexadecimal   17

Lab 1.3 Review   19

Lab 1.4: ASCII   20

ASCII Encoding   20

Lab 1.4 Review   22

Lab 1.5: Creating a File System   23

Creating a Root Folder   23

Creating Subfolders   24

Organizing a File Structure   25

Lab 1.5 Review   26

Lab 1.6: Gathering System Information   27

Hard Disk Size   27

RAM Capacity and Type   28

Processor Speed   30

Task Management   30

Lab 1.6 Review   32

Chapter 2   **Introduction to Computer Networking   34**

Lab 2.1: Connecting Computers   34

Networking Foundations   35

Peer-to-Peer Networks   35

Creating a Network Connection   38

Lab 2.1 Review   40

Lab 2.2: Network Drives   40

Shared Resources   40

Mapping a Network Drive   41

Creating a Shortcut to a Network Resource   43

Lab 2.2 Review   44

Lab 2.3: Network Types and Topologies   45

Network Types   45

Network Topologies   46

Lab 2.3 Review   49

Lab 2.4: Command-Line Interface   50

Networking from the Command Line   50

Windows Command Line   51

Mac OS Command Line   52

Linux Command Line   52

Lab 2.4 Review   54

Lab 2.5: Linux man Pages   55

Using man Pages   55

The man Page Structure   55

Lab 2.5 Review   56

Chapter 3   **Building TCP/IP Networks   58**

Lab 3.1: Network Reference Models   58

The Purpose of Reference Models   59

Modeling Communication   59

Lab 3.1 Review   60

Lab 3.2: The OSI Reference Model   60

The OSI Reference Model   60

Comparing the OSI Model Layers to Functionality   61

Using the OSI Model in Network Communication   62

Lab 3.2 Review   63

Lab 3.3: The TCP/IP Model   64

The TCP/IP Network Model   64

TCP/IP Model Protocols and Functions   64

Lab 3.3 Review   65

Lab 3.4: Data-Link Connections   66

The Data Link Layer   66

Packet Capture for Data Link Layer Connections (Wireshark)   66

Packet Capture for Data Link Layer Connections (OmniPeek)   68

Lab 3.4 Review   71

Lab 3.5: Network Resource Configuration   71

Configuring Shared Resources   72

Lab 3.5 Review   75

Chapter 4   Transmitting Bits   76

Lab 4.1: Copper Cabling   76

Copper Cable Types and Standards   77

Cable Planning and Testing   81

Lab 4.1 Review   82

Lab 4.2: Fiber-Optic Cables   83

Singe-Mode Fiber   83

Multimode Fiber   84

Lab 4.2 Review   85

Lab 4.3: Cabling Exploration   85

Creating a Cabling Hierarchy   85

Matching Cabling to Connection Needs   87

Lab 4.3 Review   90

Lab 4.4: Cable Troubleshooting   91

Identify Device Problems   91

Identify Wiring Problems   94

Creating a Troubleshooting Plan   95

Lab 4.4 Review   95

Chapter 5   Ethernet LANs   96

Lab 5.1: LAN Standards   96

Ethernet Standards   97

Ethernet Technologies   97

Lab 5.1 Review   99

Lab 5.2: MAC and IP Addresses   99

MAC Address Structure   100

Basic IP Addressing   103

Using ARP   103

Lab 5.2 Review   105

Lab 5.3: Finding Network Settings   106

Using ipconfig   106

Using ping   107

Using tracert   109

Using netstat   109

Lab 5.3 Review   110

Lab 5.4: Basic Network Troubleshooting   110

Network Troubleshooting from the Command Line   110

Lab 5.4 Review   112

Chapter 6   Wireless LANs   114

Lab 6.1: Wireless Broadcast Domains   114

Domain Types   115

Wireless Standards   115

Lab 6.1 Review   116

Lab 6.2: Identifying WLANs   117

Detecting Wireless Broadcast Domains   117

Using netsh for Wireless Networks   120

Lab 6.2 Review   124

Lab 6.3: WLAN Router Configuration   124

Wireless Routing   125

Configuring a Wireless Router   126

Wireless Domains   130

Lab 6.3 Review   130

Lab 6.4. WLAN Placement   131

Wireless AP Placement and Configuration   131

Lab 6.4 Review   132

Chapter 7   Wide-Area Networks   134

Lab 7.1: Distance Considerations   134

Crossing Distance with Signals   134

Wide-Area Network Media   135

Lab 7.1 Review   136

Lab 7.2: WAN Connections   137

WAN Connection Types   137

Dedicated Leased-Line Connections   139

Lab 7.2 Review   140

Lab 7.3: Communication Paths   141
  Determining Communication Paths   141
  Lab 7.3 Review   143
Lab 7.4: Linux Networking   143
  Linux Command-Line Networking   144
  Lab 7.4 Review   146

Chapter 8   The Internet Protocol (IP)   148

Lab 8.1: IP Addressing and Classes   148
  IPv4 Address Classes   149
  IPv4 Subnet Masks   150
  Private Address Blocks   151
  Lab 8.1 Review   152
Lab 8.2: Assigning Static IP Addresses   152
  Static IP Addressing   153
  Lab 8.2 Review   155
Lab 8.3: Routing Tables   155
  Reading a Routing Table   156
  Using the route Command   156
  Lab 8.3 Review   157
Lab 8.4: SOHO Planning   158
  Planning a Home Network   158
  SOHO Router Information   159
  Lab 8.4 Review   161

Chapter 9   The Internet   162

Lab 9.1: Broadband Internet   162
  Broadband Connections   162
  DSL Types   163
  Lab 9.1 Review   164
Lab 9.2: Networks and Subnets   165
  Calculating the Number of Hosts in a Given Network   165
  Determining Whether Computers Are on the Same Logical Network   167
  Lab 9.2 Review   169
Lab 9.3: Internet Protocol Version 6 (IPv6)   169
  IPv6 Addressing   169
  Configuring IPv6 on a Network Connection   170
  Lab 9.3 Review   172

Lab 9.4: Configuring an FTP Service   173

    Configuring FTP on a Router   173

    Lab 9.4 Review   175

Chapter 10   TCP/IP Transport   176

Lab 10.1: Transport Layer Networking Protocols   176

    Transport Control Protocol (TCP)   177

    User Datagram Protocol (UDP)   177

    Lab 10.1 Review   178

Lab 10.2: Common Network Ports   179

    Common Port Usage   179

    Lab 10.2 Review   180

Lab 10.3: Network Management   180

    Simple Network Management Protocol   181

    Lab 10.3 Review   182

Lab 10.4: Analyzing Protocols in Packet Capture   183

    Packet Capture Revisited   183

    Lab 10.4 Review   189

About the Author

Dr. Theodor Richardson is the chair of information technology at a private university where he has taught in the areas of networking, security, and web design for six years. Dr. Richardson earned his Ph.D. in computer science and engineering, with a concentration in multimedia and image processing, and a master's degree in computer science and engineering at the University of South Carolina. Prior to teaching, Dr. Richardson worked as a freelance web designer for eight years, lending his skills to companies such as United States Steel and Pixelphish Interactive. In 2006, he earned an NSA Certification in information assurance and security. Dr. Richardson has published several conference and journal papers in the area of image processing and security and has contributed to several texts on information assurance. Dr. Richardson also is the coauthor of the textbook *Secure Software Design*, published by Jones and Bartlett.

Dedication

To my dearest Katherine with love and affection. You have been my companion in adventures around the country and the world, and I hope to adventure with you for the rest of my life.

Acknowledgments

I want to thank Wendell Odom for giving me the opportunity to join him in the creation of a textbook and lab manual for beginning networking students. I want to express my many thanks to Brett Bartow, Executive Editor, for this opportunity and his support during this project. I would also like to thank Chris Cleveland, Development Editor, for his guidance and suggestions along the way.

My technical editor, Sean Wilkins, has been a fantastic help in this effort. Thank you, Sean, for all your suggestions and guidance to improve the quality and clarity of the exercises in this book. Thank you to the rest of the staff as well who have shaped this book into what you hold in your hands.

I want to thank my family for their support and the upbringing they have given me, along with a lifelong commitment to education and the freedom to explore and adventure. Thank you to my parents, Dan and Deborah, and my grandparents, Leonard and Sylvia. Thank you to Katie for your love and support through another writing project.

I would not have had this opportunity if not for the amazing guidance of my professors through the years. Thank you to Dr. Dirk Schlingmann and Dr. Song Wang for the guidance you have given me throughout the years of my education. Thank you to Dr. Jed Lyons for teaching me how to teach and how to communicate with clarity, and thank you to Dr. Duncan Buell and Dr. Manton Matthews for seeing value in me and guiding me into the wonderful world of academia.

About the Technical Reviewer

Sean Wilkins is an accomplished networking consultant for SR-W Consulting (www.sr-wconsulting.com) and has been in the field of IT since the mid-1990s, working with companies such as Cisco, Lucent, Verizon, and AT&T as well as several other private companies. Sean currently holds certifications with Cisco (CCNP/CCDP), Microsoft (MCSE), and CompTIA (A+ and Network+). He also has a Master of Science degree in information technology with a focus in network architecture and design, a Master of Science degree in organizational management, a Master's Certificate in network security, a Bachelor of Science degree in computer networking, and an Associate of Applied Science degree in computer information systems. In addition to working as a consultant, Sean spends a lot of his time as a technical writer and editor for various companies.

We Want to Hear from You!

As the reader of this book, *you* are our most important critic and commentator. We value your opinion and want to know what we're doing right, what we could do better, what areas you'd like to see us publish in, and any other words of wisdom you're willing to pass our way.

As the associate publisher for Pearson IT Certification, I welcome your comments. You can email or write me directly to let me know what you did or didn't like about this book—as well as what we can do to make our books better.

Please note that I cannot help you with technical problems related to the topic of this book. We do have a User Services group, however, where I will forward specific technical questions related to the book.

When you write, please be sure to include this book's title and author as well as your name, email address, and phone number. I will carefully review your comments and share them with the author and editors who worked on the book.

Email: feedback@pearsonitcertification.com

Mail: Dave Dusthimer
            Associate Publisher
            Pearson IT Certification
            800 East 96th Street
            Indianapolis, IN 46240 USA

Reader Services

Visit our website and register this book at www.pearsonitcertification/register for convenient access to any updates, downloads, or errata that might be available for this book.

Introduction

This book is a companion to the *Introduction to Networking* text by Wendell Odom. By wading through the labs and exercises in this book, you will have the opportunity to further explore the topics covered in Wendell's text and practice them in a hands-on manner. The constructivist approach to education states that the lessons that a person remembers best are the ones in which they use their hands to learn. This book strives to support this pedagogy by putting the skills, commands, and standards to practice with real equipment as well as critical thinking and exploration activities.

Organization

This text is organized into chapters that align with the respective chapters of the *Introduction to Networking* textbook. Each chapter is organized into labs that explore specific skills within the chapter. The chapter introduction contains a list of skills explored within the labs and an overview of the key topics of the chapter so that the student can focus on these as he or she progresses through the labs.

For each lab, the material requirements, prerequisite labs, and approximate time to completion are listed along with an overview of the skills you will explore. The lab is divided into sections that each explore a specific subtopic within the lab. The lab activities are broken down into exercises, and each lab contains a lab review that contains critical thinking and extension questions for the skills learned in the lab.

Material Requirements

This lab manual is designed for the ITT PC lab environment, which uses VMware to simulate different operating systems, but can also be performed on any Windows machine with administrative rights. The specific requirements are as follows:

- An updated VMware player
- A Windows XP PC or virtual machine with administrative rights
- A Linux OS PC, partition, or virtual machine with administrative rights
- A Cisco Linksys E4200 or equivalent wireless access point (AP)
- A USB wireless network adapter (802.11g or 802.11n)
- An active Internet connection (this can be through a LAN connection or through a wireless connection)

If a live Windows PC is being used, a Linux partition can be created through the use of the downloadable Wubi Ubuntu installer available at www.ubuntu.com/download/desktop/windows-installer. The integrated wireless network adapter can also be used in place of a USB wireless network adapter.

CompTIA Network+ Alignment

Every effort has been made in this text to align the materials to the CompTIA Network+ exam. This text does not contain all the material necessary to complete the exam, but the skills learned within it are all applicable to the exam material and will assist in study efforts toward the exam.

Introduction to Computer Data

This chapter enables you to practice the fundamentals of computing, including binary language and system resources needed to run modern operating systems and applications. The labs in this chapter are designed to reinforce concepts from Chapter 1 of your *Introduction to Networking* textbook and enable you to explore some of the more important ideas with greater depth. You learn how to translate binary values to decimal equivalents and how to translate decimal values (like the ones you encounter every day) into the binary system. You also explore the computer file system and the computer resources that comprise modern devices. At the end of this chapter, you should be able to

- Translate binary values to decimal and decimal values to binary
- Perform basic addition and logic operations on binary values
- Describe the structure of bytes and computer words
- Associate bytes to ASCII encoding
- Create a file system on a local machine
- Identify resource statistics for a computer

Lab 1.1: Reading Binary

Approximate Lab Time: 30–40 min.
Materials Needed: Paper/Pencil, Microsoft Excel

This lab is focused on exploring the binary numbering system. In particular, you will practice breaking down the decimal numbering system with which you are familiar and converting between this system and the binary system used by computers. You will practice the conversion between these two systems and construct a simple spreadsheet to automate conversions, compile a lab report of the solutions to the assigned exercises, and include a review of the work necessary to arrive at the solution.

Breaking Down Decimal Values

To begin this activity, you must first understand how the decimal numbering system works. This system is also called the *base 10 system* because each digit represents a power of 10. Take the number 127, for example. From right to left, the digits are organized based on powers of 10 such that there are seven values of 10^0, two values of 10^1, plus one value of 10^2. You know these as the ones, tens, and hundreds places, respectively. You can see this breakdown in Figure 1-1.

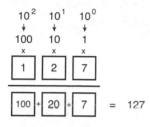

FIGURE 1-1   Breakdown of 127 (Base 10)

> **NOTE:** Any number raised to the power of 0 is equal to 1, so $10^0 = 1$ just like $2^0 = 1$.
>
> The available digits in any numbering system range from 0 to the base value minus 1; in the case of base 10, this gives us the possible digit values from 0 to 9.

This type of breakdown is essential to understanding binary systems. By using only the available digits and knowing the value of each digit placement, you can start to represent numbers without the type of mapping shown in Figure 1-1. The goal of this lab is to allow you to read binary (or base 2) values with the same fluency that you use for decimal (or base 10) values.

Exercise 1.1.1

Create a mapping similar to Figure 1-1 for the decimal number 2931 using either paper and pencil or a Word document.

Mapping Binary Values

The binary (base 2) system used by computing systems is based on the fact that electronic signals have two states of existence: on or off. The off state is equal to 0, and the on state is equal to 1. By combining several of these signals together in a pattern, you can represent more complex values in a similar manner to representing values in the decimal system. Each binary digit is called a bit, and inside a computer, each bit represents one signal state. Creating binary mappings like Figure 1-1 is equivalent to each column having a value of yes (1) or no (0) for whether the column heading should be added to the final result.

> **NOTE:** Base 2 (binary) values are often denoted with the subscript 2, indicating the base system used for the number, such as 1011_2. When no subscript is present, it can be assumed that the value is in the base 10 (decimal) system.

Figure 1-2 shows a breakdown of the binary value 101_2. This is similar to the mapping created in Figure 1-1 except the base value of the mapping has changed from 10 to 2. The resulting sum is shown in decimal, indicating how you can easily read binary numbers as decimal values.

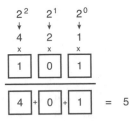

FIGURE 1-2   Breakdown of 101 (Base 2)

Exercise 1.1.2

Create a mapping similar to Figure 1-2 for the binary number 110_2 using either paper and pencil or a Word document.

_____

_____

_____

Exercise 1.1.3

Create a mapping similar to Figure 1-2 for the binary number 11_2 using either paper and pencil or a Word document.

_____

_____

_____

Binary Conversion

Binary values can be converted to the decimal equivalent by following the mapping procedures outlined in Figure 1-2. As you should see from Exercise 1.1.3, you can expand this mapping to include as many digits as needed simply by adding powers of 2 to the left. The leftmost power of 2 is always one less than the number of digits in the value, so for a four-digit binary number, the highest power of 2 to the left will be 3. For example, for the four-digit binary number 1100_2, the expanded mapping is shown in Figure 1-3.

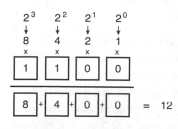

FIGURE 1-3 Breakdown of 1100 (Base 2)

Keep in mind that most binary values are grouped in sets of four or eight digits (this idea is related to binary storage in words and bytes, which will be explored later), where the leftmost unoccupied bits are set at 0 (called leading 0s). For these exercises, you should use the smallest multiple of four digits that can accommodate the result. To illustrate this, the number 11_2 contains only 2 bits but would be stored as 4 bits, as shown in Figure 1-4. Similarly, the number 10001_2 has only 5 bits but would be stored as 8 bits.

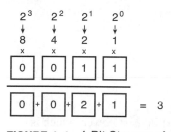

FIGURE 1-4 4-Bit Storage of 11 (Base 2)

Exercise 1.1.4

Create an expanded mapping similar to Figure 1-3 for the binary number 10010_2 using either paper and pencil or a Word document.

_____

_____

_____

_____

Exercise 1.1.5

Create an expanded mapping similar to Figure 1-3 for the binary number 11100010_2 using either paper and pencil or a Word document.

_____

_____

_____

_____

Decimal Conversion

One of the easiest ways to convert a decimal number to binary is through repeated subtraction. The first step is to list powers of 2 from right to left until you reach one that is larger than the decimal value you want to convert (for the number 15, the list would be 16 8 4 2 1). Now move through the list from left to right, placing a 1 beneath the first power of 2 less than the decimal value you want to convert and subtract that amount from the decimal value. You should repeat this process moving to the right until the decimal result is 0. An example of this (omitting the powers of 2 larger than the decimal value to convert) is shown for the number 233 in Figure 1-5.

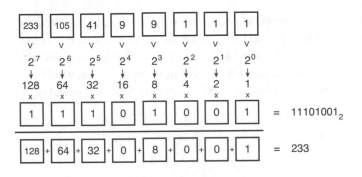

FIGURE 1-5   Conversion of 233 (Base 10) to Binary

The steps to complete this exercise in conversion are as follows:

STEP 1. 2^7 is the smallest power of 2 less than 233 ($2^8 = 256$ is the next-highest power, which is greater).

STEP 2.   For 2^7: 233 is greater than 128, so the leftmost bit is 1. The decimal result is $233 - 128 = 105$.

STEP 3.   For 2^6: 105 is greater than 64, so the next bit to the right is 1. The decimal result is $105 - 64 = 41$.

STEP 4.   For 2^5: 41 is greater than 32, so the next bit to the right is 1. The decimal result is $41 - 32 = 9$.

STEP 5.   For 2^4: 9 is less than 16, so the next bit to the right is 0. The decimal result remains 9.

STEP 6.   For 2^3: 9 is greater than 8, so the next bit to the right is 1. The decimal result is $9 - 8 = 1$.

STEP 7.   For 2^2: 1 is less than 4, so the next bit to the right is 0. The decimal result remains 1.

STEP 8.   For 2^1: 1 is less than 2, so the next bit to the right is 0. The decimal result remains 1.

STEP 9.   For 2^0: 1 is equal to 1, so the rightmost bit is 1. The decimal result is $1 - 1 = 0$, so we are finished with the conversion.

Exercise 1.1.6

Using the example in Figure 1-5 and the steps that followed, create a binary conversion for the decimal value 156.

_____

_____

_____

_____

Exercise 1.1.7

Using the example in Figure 1-5 and the steps that followed, create a binary conversion for the decimal value 255.

_____

_____

_____

_____

Exercise 1.1.8

Using the example in Figure 1-5 and the steps that followed, create a binary conversion for the decimal value 200.

_____

_____

_____

_____

Creating a Conversion Worksheet

For this exercise, you will create a simple Excel spreadsheet for converting 8-bit binary values to decimal. This will be a helpful reference for the coming labs, where you will explore ASCII encoding and hexadecimal values. You can see an example of the spreadsheet you will create in Figure 1-6.

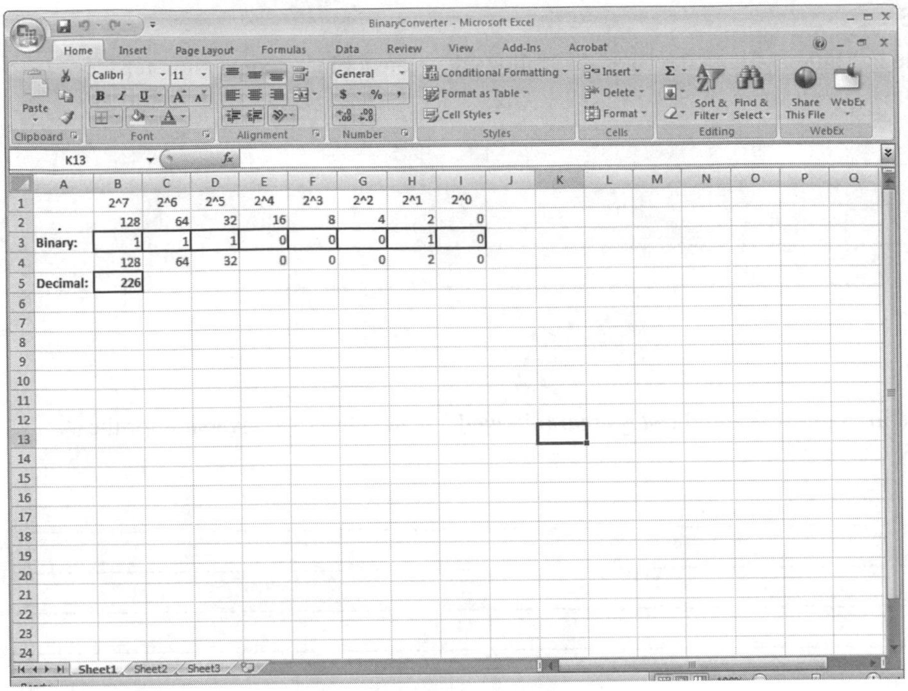

FIGURE 1-6   Excel 8-Bit Binary Converter

To begin, open Microsoft Excel and create a new blank workbook (from the File menu) and save your document as BinaryConverter.xlsx. In the top row of the new spreadsheet, beginning with cell B1, enter the powers of 2 for each bit (represented as 2^7 for 2^7); this will be your placeholder for the bits you will enter.

> **NOTE:** In Excel, each cell is referenced by the letter of the column and then the number of the row, so B3 represents the intersection of column B and row 3.

In cell B2, begin entering the numerical values for the equivalent powers of 2 in row 1. You will know that the number has been stored as a number because it will align to the right in the cell, whereas normal text aligns to the left.

In cell A3, enter the term **Binary:** and then select the cells from B3 to I3. With the cells selected, add a border to the cells (using the Borders icon on the Font panel of the Home ribbon); this is where you will enter your binary values for conversion.

In cell B4, you will enter your first formula. In this case, you will enter **=B2*B3** and then press **Enter**. Right now, the cell should show the value of 0 because cell B3 is empty. You can copy this formula to the remaining cells by clicking inside cell B4 and selecting the lower-right grip point on the box around cell B4; with the mouse button held down, drag the grip point over to cell I4. You can see the grip point in Figure 1-7 (you will know it is selected when the mouse pointer becomes a black crosshair).

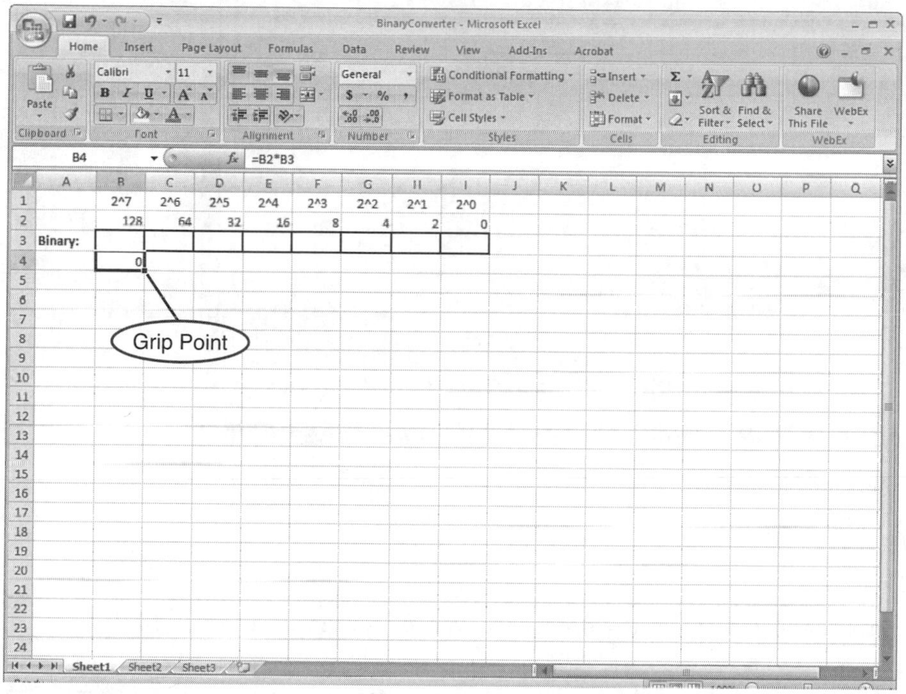

FIGURE 1-7   Grip Point to Copy Cell Contents in Excel 2010

In cell A5, enter the term **Decimal:**. In cell B5, enter the formula **=SUM(B4:I4)** and press **Enter**. You should add a border around this cell as well. Save your work.

Now, when you enter binary digits in the marked cells B3 through I3, the decimal equivalent will populate in cell B5. You should try it with the example 11100010_2 (entering either 1 or 0 in each cell as the bit value) and make sure that you get the result 226 in cell B5.

For your reference in case you need help, the formulas are shown in the correct cells in Figure 1-8. Remember that if you have less than 8 bits in the value, place the rightmost bit in the 2^0 column and work your way to the left; populate any empty bits with leading 0s.

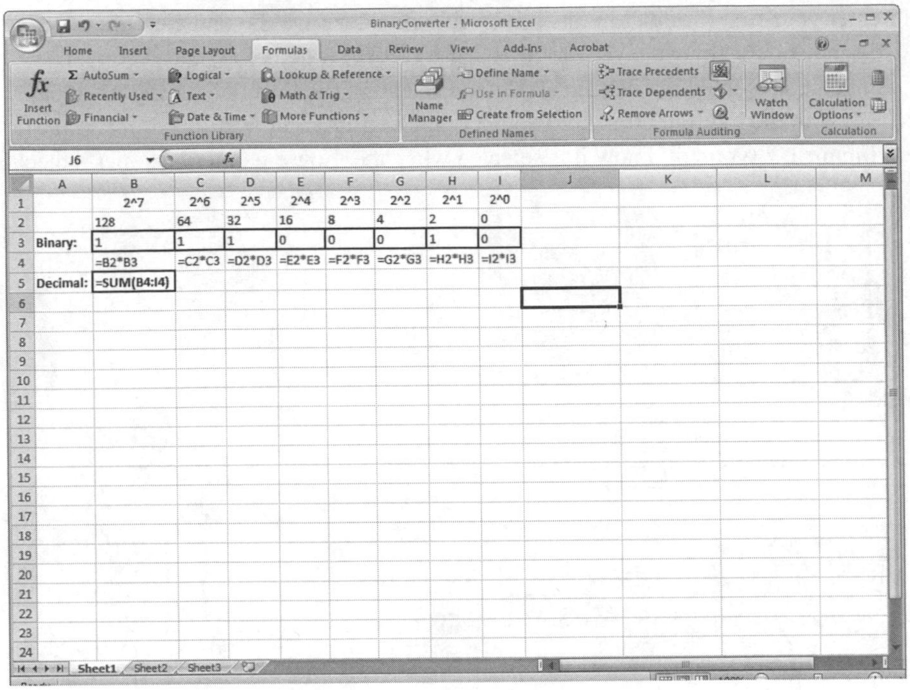

FIGURE 1-8 Formulas for Binary Converter

Exercise 1.1.9

Using the binary converter document, create a decimal conversion for the binary value 1001_2.

_____

_____

Exercise 1.1.10

Using the binary converter document, create a decimal conversion for the binary value 10111001_2.

_____

_____

Exercise 1.1.11

Using the binary converter document, create a decimal conversion for the binary value 101111_2.

_____

_____

Exercise 1.1.12

Using the binary converter document, create a decimal conversion for the binary value 10000001_2.

_____

_____

Lab 1.1 Review

1. Convert the decimal value 127 to binary. Explain the process of conversion that you used.

_____

_____

2. Explain why the values 10_2 and 0010_2 are equivalent.

_____

_____

3. Based on the breakdown of the decimal and binary systems in this lab, describe the available digit values and the first four digits of a base 5 numbering system. You can use the binary system as a reference, where the available digit values are 0 and 1 and the first four digits are 1, 2, 4, and 8.

_____

4. Using the Internet and the Help files in Excel, explain why creating a converter from decimal to binary would be more difficult to construct. Hint: you should consider the conditional evaluation of whether the decimal value remaining is larger than the binary digit value.

_____

_____

_____

Lab 1.2: Binary Math and Logic

Approximate Lab Time: 20–30 min.
Prerequisite: Lab 1.1
Materials Needed: Pencil/Paper

Now that you have an understanding of the binary numbering system, you can begin to practice the mathematical and logical operations that can be performed on two or more binary values. While there is a wide array of computations that can be performed, it will suffice for the purpose of networking and addressing to explore the concepts of binary addition and the logical AND and OR operators. Compile a lab report of the solutions to the assigned exercises, and include a review of the work necessary to arrive at the solution.

Binary Addition

Binary addition works just like addition in the decimal system. Fortunately, the addition system in binary has only four possible results for adding two bits together:

1. $0 + 0 = 0_2$
2. $0 + 1 = 1_2$
3. $1 + 0 = 1_2$
4. $1 + 1 = 10_2$

In case 4, the addition exceeds the value of a single digit, so the result must carry over to the next bit to the left. This same result can be extrapolated to cover larger bit-by-bit additions. When you expand the addition, you must also consider the case of 1+1 with another 1 carried over. In this case, the result for the bit will be 1 and the carry value will be 1 ($1 + 1 + 1 = 11_2$). You can see a mapping of this type of addition with carry values in Figure 1-9.

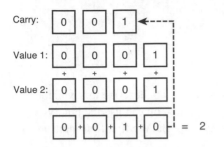

FIGURE 1-9 Binary Addition Example

Exercise 1.2.1

Using Figure 1-9 as an example, determine the result of adding 110_2 and 1001_2.

_____

_____

_____

_____

Exercise 1.2.2

Using Figure 1-9 as an example, determine the result of adding 110_2 and 101_2.

_____

_____

_____

_____

Exercise 1.2.3

Using Figure 1-9 as an example, determine the result of adding 111_2 and 111_2.

_____

_____

_____

_____

AND/OR Logic

Two additional logic operators are used frequently on binary values in networking. These are the AND and OR operators. The OR operator compares the two bits given as input and produces a 1 if either of them is 1 (or if both of them are 1) and a 0 otherwise. This is best illustrated using a truth table, as shown in Figure 1-10. You might encounter other logic truth tables where the 1s and 0s are represented as True or False values, respectively (which gives the truth table its name), showing all possible results for the logical combination of the input.

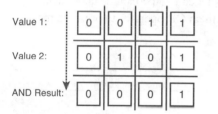

FIGURE 1-10   OR Binary Truth Table

The AND logical operator is another tool for combining binary values into a single result. The AND operator only produces a result of 1 when both values are 1; otherwise, it produces a 0 result. You can see the truth table for the AND operator on two binary values in Figure 1-11. Just like binary addition, the results are applied on a bit-by-bit basis, so 111 OR 011 = 111_2 because each digit contains a 1 in either of the two values. Similarly, 111 AND 011 = 011_2. Another logical operator called NOT will reverse the bits of a value, so NOT 101 = 010_2.

> **NOTE:** These binary operations might seem difficult, but understanding these is necessary for making use of IP addresses later in this text, particularly the AND and NOT operators, which can define the network and host portions of an IP address. You will see these operators again in Chapter 8, "The Internet Protocol (IP)," through Chapter 10, "TCP/IP Transport."

FIGURE 1-11   AND Binary Truth Table

Exercise 1.2.4

Determine the result of 100_2 OR 011_2.

Exercise 1.2.5

Determine the result of 111_2 AND 100_2.

Exercise 1.2.6

Determine the result of NOT 1001_2.

Binary Operations Practice

Now that you have a basic understanding of how binary addition and logic work, you will practice these skills and start to critically analyze the results of these operations.

Exercise 1.2.7

Using binary addition, what is the result of $1010_2 + 10_2$? Using binary addition, how would you repeatedly increment a number by 2?

_____

_____

Exercise 1.2.8

Using the AND operator, what is the result of 1100_2 AND 1111_2? What can you conclude about using AND on any value with a string of 1s?

_____

_____

Exercise 1.2.9

Using the OR operator, what is the result of 1100_2 OR 1111_2? What can you conclude about using OR on any value with a string of 1s? What value can you use with an OR operator to preserve the other input number in the logical equation?

_____

_____

Lab 1.2 Review

1. Determine the result of $10010000_2 + 1101110_2$. Show the mapping that you created to solve this addition problem.

_____

_____

_____

_____

2. Determine the result of 11001100_2 AND 11111100_2. Show the mapping or truth table that you used to solve this logic problem.

_____

_____

_____

_____

3. Determine the result of 11001100_2 OR 11111100_2. Show the mapping or truth table that you used to solve this logic problem.

_____

_____

_____

_____

4. Using parentheses in binary works just like it does in decimal, where the operation inside the parentheses should be performed first. With this rule, determine the result of NOT(11001100_2 AND 11111100_2). Show the steps, mapping, or truth table that you used to solve this logic problem.

_____

_____

Lab 1.3: Bit and Byte Structure

Approximate Lab Time: 20–30 min.
Prerequisite: Lab 1.1
Materials Needed: Paper/Pencil, Microsoft Excel, Internet

This lab furthers the analysis of the binary language from Lab 1.1 and examines how it is stored in a computing system. It will also introduce the hexadecimal system, which can be used as a shorthand system for representing binary. You should construct a lab report of the solutions and any supporting work for the assigned exercises throughout the lab.

Byte Construction

A single bit is not sufficient to represent much information. In fact, it can only represent two states, such as true and false, yes and no, 0 and 1, or on and off. However, as you have seen in the previous lab, you can use the binary language to represent longer numerical values by combining bits into a sequence of binary digits. The most common form of this is the byte, which consists of 8 consecutive binary digits. This is typically the smallest amount of information that can be stored in a computing system (though some programming languages and systems allow the use of a nibble, which is half of a byte or 4 consecutive binary digits).

Bytes can be chained together sequentially to represent even more complex information. For example, 2 bytes can be read as one sequence to allow the storage of numeric values up to 65535 (or $2^{16} - 1$). You can see an example of this in Figure 1-12.

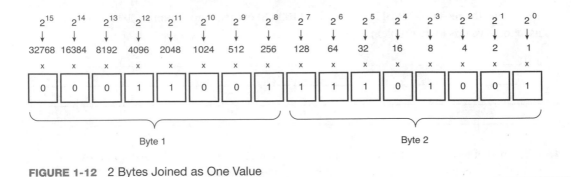

FIGURE 1-12   2 Bytes Joined as One Value

Exercise 1.3.1

What is the decimal value of Byte 1 by itself? What is the decimal value of Byte 2 by itself?

Exercise 1.3.2

What is the decimal equivalent of the binary sequence in Figure 1-12 (the combined sequence of Byte 1 and Byte 2 as a single decimal value)? How does this compare to the individual values of Byte 1 and Byte 2?

Byte Storage Capacity

One important application of sequential binary digits coupled into bytes is the word size of the computer. A *word* in a computer is the preferred number of bits that can be moved at once. This is typically equal to the register size of the computer's processor. If a computer has a 32-bit processor, it will have a word size of 32 bits, or 4 bytes. Similarly, modern 64-bit processors have a word size of 64 bits, or 8 bytes. You can access smaller amounts of information within the computer word, but when a computer addresses memory, it divides the full amount of available storage space into sequentially numbered words. Because the word size can vary from machine to machine, the storage space is often defined as the number of bytes that can be stored.

Because of the vast number of bytes of information that can be stored in a modern computer system, it is necessary to recognize and use shorthand to represent these large volumes. For this reason, storage sizes are often represented by increments of 2^{10}, or 1024. Table 1-1 shows the common abbreviations for different storage capacities.

Table 1-1   Common Abbreviations for Storage Capacity

Abbreviation	Definition
Kilobyte (KB)	1024 bytes
Megabyte (MB)	1024 kilobytes
Gigabyte (GB)	1024 megabytes
Terabyte (TB)	1024 gigabytes

Based on this system, a device that can store 2 kilobytes (2 KB) of data can store 2048 bytes of data. A storage device that can hold 5 MB of data can hold 5120 KB of data, or 5,242,880 bytes of data. For ease of estimation, you can use 1000 as an approximation for determining storage capacity, but you should be careful in technical work to use the actual 2^{10} (or 1024) as the real value.

> **NOTE:** Recognize the capitalization of the B in the KB abbreviation. When the B is capitalized, it represents bytes, but when it is lowercase, it represents bits. This becomes important later when discussing network speeds, which are often given in kilobits or megabits transferred per second versus the kilobytes and megabytes of data storage available.

Exercise 1.3.3

Given a device with a storage capacity of 120 MB, how many bytes can be stored on this device? Show your calculations.

Exercise 1.3.4

Given a computer with a disk capacity of 16 GB and a word size of 32 bits, how many words can be stored on the disk? Show your calculations.

Hexadecimal

Hexadecimal is another numbering system you will encounter in computing and networking. This is a base 16 system (derived from *hexa*, which means six, and *decimal*, which means ten). It is more difficult to convert decimal numbers to hexadecimal than it is to convert them to binary. The true value of hexadecimal, though, is its use as shorthand for representing binary values. A single hexadecimal digit is equivalent to 4 binary digits. This means that rather than using 8 binary digits to express the value of a byte, you can use two hexadecimal digits to express the same value.

Because the decimal numbering system we use has only the digit values of 0 through 9, it is necessary to add additional symbols to represent the remaining possible digit values in the base 16 system. To address this, the letters a through f are used to represent the values 10 through 15, respectively. Table 1-2 shows the complete conversion chart between hexadecimal digit values and the decimal and binary values.

Table 1-2   Conversion Chart for Hexadecimal, Decimal, and Binary

Hexadecimal Value	Decimal Value	Binary Value
0	0	0000
1	1	0001
2	2	0010
3	3	0011
4	4	0100
5	5	0101
6	6	0110
7	7	0111
8	8	1000
9	9	1001
a	10	1010
b	11	1011
c	12	1100
d	13	1101
e	14	1110
f	15	1111

From this chart, you can see how to represent binary information quickly using hexadecimal. For example, a byte containing the binary value 11000011_2 can be represented using the hexadecimal value $c3_{16}$ by substituting one hexadecimal digit for each set of four binary digits. Figure 1-13 shows the process of decomposing binary values to hexadecimal. The reverse process works the same way, where dc_{16} is equivalent to 11011100_2 because d_{16} is equal to 1101_2 and c_{16} is equal to 1100_2.

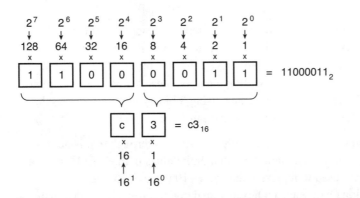

FIGURE 1-13   Converting a Byte to Hexadecimal

If the binary value contains a number of digits that are not divisible by 4, you can pad it to a number of digits that are divisible by 4 by adding leading 0s. For example, 10011_2 (which has five digits that cannot be represented in groups of four) is equivalent to 00010011_2 (which contains eight digits that can be represented by two groups of four). The latter of these values can easily be represented by 13_{16}, where 1_{16} is equal to 000_{12} and 3_{16} is equal to 0011_2. Converting from decimal to hexadecimal is a more complex process, and it is often much easier to convert the decimal value to binary and then use the result to convert to the hexadecimal value.

The hexadecimal numbering system is common shorthand for binary, particularly in computer addressing. This is common in addressing on a local machine (such as determining a hard drive sector) and in networking for defining a MAC address (the physical address of a network interface card, which is covered to a larger extent later in the book).

Exercise 1.3.5

Represent the binary value 110110_2 in hexadecimal. Show the steps of conversion that you used.

_____

_____

Exercise 1.3.6

Represent the hexadecimal value $f6_{16}$ in binary and decimal. Show the steps of conversion that you used.

_____

_____

Lab 1.3 Review

1. Explain why it is important to know how many system words will fit in a primary storage device on a computer (such as the hard drive).

   _____

   _____

2. Explain why more information can be contained in multiple bytes joined together than in a single byte.

   _____

   _____

   _____

3. Explain why it is more difficult to convert a decimal value to hexadecimal than it is to convert it to binary.

   _____

   _____

   _____

4. Convert the number 327 to hexadecimal. Show the conversion steps you have taken. Hint: It is easier to convert the value to binary first and use the binary result to convert to hexadecimal.

_____

_____

_____

_____

Lab 1.4: ASCII

Approximate Lab Time: 15–25 min.
Prerequisite: Lab 1.3
Materials Needed: Paper/Pencil, Microsoft Word or Excel, Internet

This lab extends the concepts of the data that can be stored in binary. You will explore the ASCII encoding system for text processing. This is the standard format for plain text, and it will give you an idea of how other encoding systems can be developed to store different types of data on a computer. You should construct a lab report of the solutions and any supporting work for the assigned exercises throughout the lab.

ASCII Encoding

Binary can be used to directly represent numerical information, but there is a clear need to represent different types of data, such as text. To accomplish this, an encoding system has to be defined to equate the binary value to the data it should represent. One of the most common encoding systems for representing text is the American Standard Code for Information Interchange (ASCII or US-ASCII), developed in the 1960s. This system is comprised of 128 characters, including 95 printing characters and 33 control characters. This means that it can be represented using 7 bits of information. When ASCII is stored on a computer, each character occupies the lesser 7 bits of a byte (meaning that it has a single leading 0). Table 1-3 is a subset of the ASCII encoding system, showing the values corresponding to letters.

Table 1-3   ASCII Conversion Chart for Letters

Hex	Character	Hex	Character
41	A	61	a
42	B	62	b
43	C	63	c
44	D	64	d
45	E	65	e
46	F	66	f
47	G	67	g
48	H	68	h

Hex	Character	Hex	Character
49	I	69	i
4a	J	6a	j
4b	K	6b	k
4c	L	6c	l
4d	M	6d	m
4e	N	6e	n
4f	O	6f	o
50	P	70	p
51	Q	71	q
52	R	72	r
53	S	73	s
54	T	74	t
55	U	75	u
56	V	76	v
57	W	77	w
58	X	78	x
59	Y	79	y
5a	Z	7a	z

Note in the chart that ASCII uses different values for uppercase and lowercase letters. There are a variety of ASCII codes for characters that do not display on the screen as well as codes for symbols and a blank space. Programs like Notepad, which stores text only (without formatting), record ASCII encoding directly in the file, storing binary on the computer and interpreting the binary as text to display on the computer monitor for you to read.

Exercise 1.4.1

What is the ASCII hexadecimal code for a blank space? Why is it necessary to represent a blank space as a separate character in text?

Exercise 1.4.2

Using Microsoft Word or Excel, create a chart similar to Table 1-3 for the hexadecimal codes for the numbers from 0 through 9.

Exercise 1.4.3

What are the binary and decimal values of the ASCII letter K? Show the steps of the conversion.

_____

_____

_____

_____

While ASCII is typically used to store one character per byte, it does not occupy a full byte of information (using only the lesser 7 bits with a leading 0). Most computer systems use the remaining codes to extend the ASCII system to include other unusual characters. ASCII was the standard for use on the World Wide Web until 2007, when it was replaced by UTF-8. UTF-8 retains the encoding equivalent of ASCII for the first 128 values (so a capital letter A in ASCII has the same encoding as a capital letter A in UTF-8). For this portion of the lab, you will use the web to explore different encoding schemes for text as directed by the exercises.

Exercise 1.4.4

Use the web to explore the origin of the Universal Character Set (UCS)—ISO/IEC 10646—and explain why it was developed. Compare and contrast this system with ASCII. What is the relationship of ASCII to the UCS encoding?

_____

_____

_____

Exercise 1.4.5

Use the web to explore the application of UTF-8 text encoding. What features are provided by UTF-8 that are not provided by ASCII? Why was it chosen to replace ASCII as the standard for the web?

_____

_____

_____

_____

Lab 1.4 Review

1. Using the ASCII encoding scheme, write your name (including the space between your first and last name) in hexadecimal. How much memory would it take to store your name if each ASCII character occupied a byte?

_____

_____

2. Using a word size of 64 bits, how much memory space is wasted by the leading 0 used to store 256 ASCII characters each in individual bytes? Justify your answer.

_____

_____

_____

3. What is the binary equivalent of the word *NETWORK* using ASCII encoding?

_____

_____

Lab 1.5: Creating a File System

Approximate Lab Time: 10–15 min.
Materials Needed: PC Lab (Windows, Linux, or Mac OS)

For this lab, you will explore basic memory organization and retrieval in a computer system. This will require the use of a PC with Windows, Linux, or Mac OS. You will be using the GUI for this assignment, so you can choose whichever operating system you prefer to use. You should construct a lab report of the solutions and any supporting work for the assigned exercises throughout the lab.

Creating a Root Folder

Modern operating systems do not organize files sequentially. Typically, the operating system (or OS for short) will find a suitable location on the storage disk (the computer's long-term memory) at which to store a file and then retain a reference to the address where the file starts. This is not a sufficient interface for a user to find the information that he or she wants to locate. To allow a more logical organization for human use, the operating system maintains a file structure based on folders. Each drive (a partition of a storage disk indicated by a letter) on the system will have its own file structure. You can start exploring this on a Windows machine by double-clicking the Computer icon on the desktop and selecting the C: drive. When you enter the C: drive (the default name for the main drive used by the computer to store information), you will see a variety of system folders. You can even create a new folder in this location (though it is not recommended) by right-clicking inside the window, selecting New, and then choosing Folder, as demonstrated in Figure 1-14.

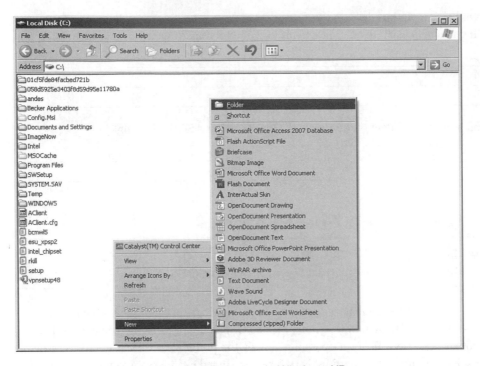

FIGURE 1-14 Example C: Directory Structure in Windows XP

Each of these folders is the root of its own tree of subfolders and files. The files and folders within this root folder can be located anywhere in memory, but the operating system will maintain a record of where they are located in storage if you need to open or execute any of them. When you move a folder or file from location to location in the file structure, you do not change its physical location in memory, just the reference to where it should be connected in relation to the rest of the file system. To understand the relationship between folders in a directory, you will create a new root folder for the first exercise.

Exercise 1.5.1

On the desktop of your operating system, create a new folder called Classes. Open the C: drive and locate the path through the subfolders from the root directory C: to get to your Classes folder. This path will differ slightly depending on the operating system. Record the navigation path to get to your new Classes folder. Hint: Most directory structures that include the desktop of a computer involve finding a folder for users and selecting the correct user.

Creating Subfolders

Within each folder that you create, you can save files and you can create new folders. Each of these will create a link in your operating system between the root folder and the subfolders or files that it contains. To demonstrate this, you should open the Classes folder you created in the last exercise and create four new subfolders called Computing, English, Math, and Networking. Each of these new folders has a reference in the OS filing structure. You can see an example of the new folders in Figure 1-15.

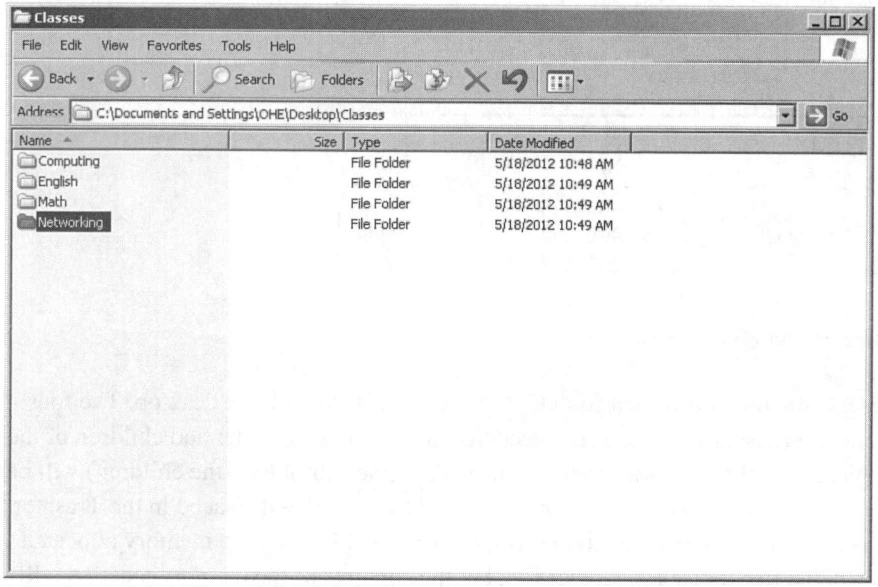

FIGURE 1-15   Sample Subfolders

Open a text-editing program such as Notepad or Emacs. (To open Notepad in Windows, click the Start button, choose All Programs, Accessories, and then choose Notepad.) Create a new file, type your name, and save it to your Classes folder with the name myname.txt. The file now has a reference in the OS to the folder in which it is stored, and the OS knows the address in memory that contains the file.

Exercise 1.5.2

Open the Classes folder you created and move the myname.txt file to the Networking folder. What has happened to the OS reference to the location of the file myname.txt? What has happened to the physical storage location of myname.txt in memory?

Organizing a File Structure

File structures in a modern OS are organized as a hierarchy, where each subfolder is a child of its root folder. You can see an example of this hierarchy for the folders you have created in Figure 1-16. Whenever you create new subfolders, you will add children to the root folder under which they were created. Using this model, you can plan a file structure to organize your work in this class or for your entire curriculum. Subfolders at the same level are considered peers, and despite the ability to organize them by various attributes, they are all considered equal.

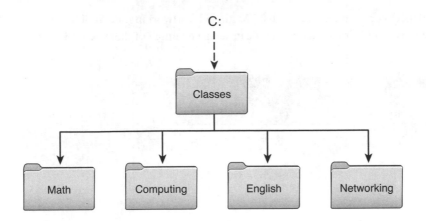

FIGURE 1-16   Example Folder Hierarchies

The dotted line represents the folder traversal from C: to the Classes folder on the desktop. The four folders contained inside the Classes folder are all considered siblings to each other and children of the Classes folder in the hierarchy. If the Classes folder is deleted, all the subfolders (the children) will be deleted along with any subfolders they contain. If the Classes folder is deleted (placed in the Trash or Recycle Bin and then emptied) while myname.txt is within it or its subfolders, the memory allocated to the file will be considered free to use for another file, but the contents of the memory location will not be overwritten until another file is stored at that location.

Exercise 1.5.3

Inside the Networking folder, create a new set of folders for your labs and assignments. You should add at least five subfolders. Diagram the hierarchy that now exists from the root Classes folder.

_____

Exercise 1.5.4

Disk fragmentation occurs when files are deleted from memory but that space is not used to store another file. Use the web to identify issues that disk fragmentation can cause for computer performance. Will changing your file structure affect the fragmentation of the disk? Justify your answer.

_____
_____
_____
_____

Lab 1.5 Review

1. Why is it necessary to plan a file structure carefully? What can happen if it is too loosely organized or too detailed?

_____
_____
_____

2. Locate the path of folders to the text application you used to create the myname.txt file. How does this differ from the path taken to reach the desktop?

_____

_____

_____

3. When you defragment a disk, what happens to the memory references maintained by the OS? What happens to the file system organization? You can use the web to research your answer. Make sure that you justify your argument.

_____

_____

Lab 1.6: Gathering System Information

Approximate Lab Time: 20–30 min.
Materials Needed: PC Lab (Windows, Linux, or Mac OS)

For this lab, you will be gathering system information on the hardware that comprises a computer system. All the major operating systems (Windows, Linux, and Mac OS) have this system information available, and you will need to use two different operating systems to complete the assigned exercises. This will allow you to compare the allocated system resources. You should construct a lab report of the solutions and any supporting work for the assigned exercises throughout the lab.

Hard Disk Size

The capacity and available space on a hard disk is a common consideration for computing. The larger the disk, the more data you can store. Typically, the hard drive is used to store the operating system, all installed software, and user files. As the size of the drive increases, so does the address space required to get to all the information and the time it takes for retrieval of the information. However, as technology improves, these differences compared to the storage size increases are becoming minimal. It is always beneficial to be able to determine the amount of space that you have remaining on your hard drive.

For Windows, you can open the Computer icon on the desktop and view a list of mounted drives (indicated by letters) and the capacity and available space for each. In Windows XP, you can access this information by right-clicking the C: drive and selecting Properties. You can see an example of this in Figure 1-17.

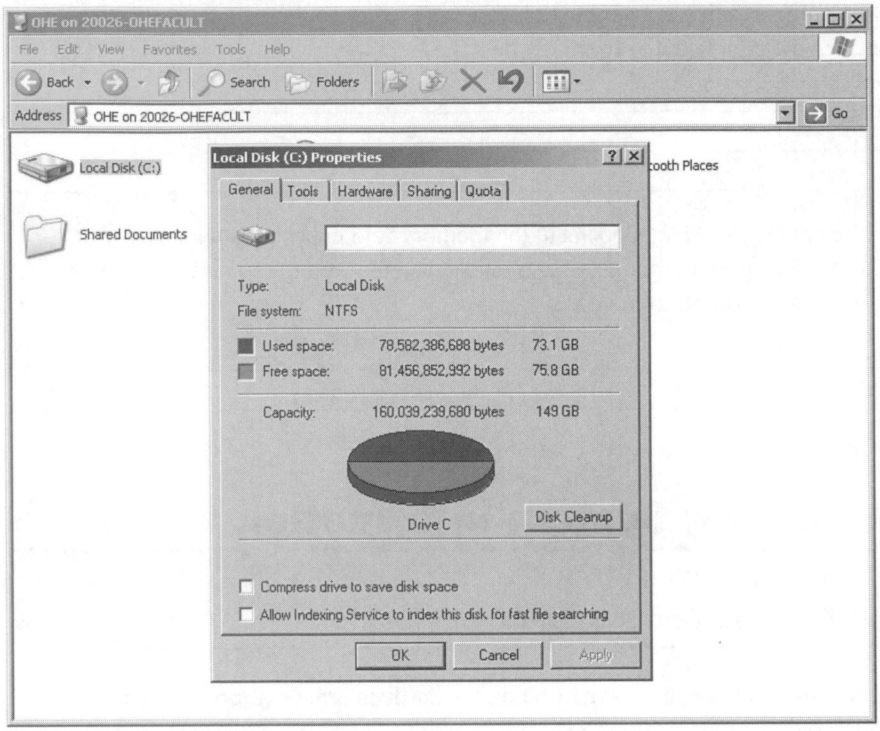

FIGURE 1-17   Example Hard Drive Space in Windows XP

Exercise 1.6.1

Record the amount of space you have available and how much total space you have on your Windows hard drive.

Exercise 1.6.2

Using a Linux or Mac OS computer, determine the amount of space you have available and how much total space you have on the hard drive. On Mac OS X, you can get this information by right-clicking the MacintoshHD icon on the desktop and selecting Get Info. On a Linux machine, you can type **df -h** at the command-line interface.

RAM Capacity and Type

The random-access memory (RAM) of a machine is chip-based memory storage into which active program instructions and data are passed from the hard drive that can be readily accessed by the central processing unit (CPU). RAM allows a machine to operate on data with minimal lag time to get results rather than the slower process of storing and retrieving information using the hard drive. RAM can typically be changed in a computer system through removable chipsets. Even most laptops have the ability to customize the amount of RAM installed after purchase. The more RAM you have installed, the better your computer will perform and the better it can handle multitasking.

In Windows, this information is part of the System information. You can access this by opening the Control Panel (from the **Start** menu, choose **Settings** in Windows XP) and double-clicking the System icon. This will open a new window with basic device information, such as the OS version, the processor information, and the amount and type of RAM installed. You can see an example of this window for Windows XP in Figure 1-18.

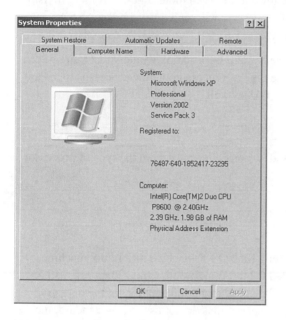

FIGURE 1-18   Sample System Information for Windows XP

Exercise 1.6.3

Locate the system information for your Windows machine and record the amount of RAM you have installed.

Exercise 1.6.4

Locate the amount of RAM you have available on either a Mac OS X machine or a Linux machine. Compare this to the RAM allocated for the Windows machine. On a Mac OS X computer, open the MacintoshHD directory, open the Applications folder, open the Utilities folder, and then choose System Profiler to find the amount of RAM installed. On a Linux machine, you can use the **free** command to display the amount of memory available and the amount in use; to get the result in megabytes, use the **free -m** command at the command-line interface.

Processor Speed

The processor speed is the other key element to system performance. The speed associated with the processor is typically in hertz (Hz) (cycles per second). This is the number of clock cycles per second and determines how much processing can be done. Keep in mind that not every action can be completed in a single clock cycle, such as multiplication and the even more time-consuming division operation. Still, a faster speed and greater number of processors will tend toward better system performance, though this is also tied to the system RAM.

On a Windows machine, this information is part of the System Information window that you opened to determine the amount of RAM on the machine. The type of processor and the processor speed are both given in this window. You can see this in Figure 1-18 as well.

Exercise 1.6.5

Access the System Information window on your Windows machine and record the type of processor and the processor speed for the computer.

Exercise 1.6.6

Locate the processor type and speed installed on either a Mac OS X machine or a Linux machine. Compare this to the processor type and speed installed for the Windows machine. On a Mac OS X computer, select the Apple menu and choose **About This Mac** to get information on the operating system, processor, and processor speed. Though some incarnations do not use this as standard, the most common way to access CPU information on a Linux machine is to use the command **cat/proc/cpuinfo**.

Task Management

Another important utility to be able to access on your local machine is the Task Manager. This utility will allow you to examine the processes that are running on your machine and the amount of processing power, memory, and network traffic they are using. This becomes increasingly important when you are monitoring your network activity in later chapters. The Windows Task Manager utility allows you to view this information in different tabs. To start the Task Manager, press **Ctrl+Alt+Delete** and select the **Task Manager** option in the screen that appears. You can see an example of this utility in Figure 1-19.

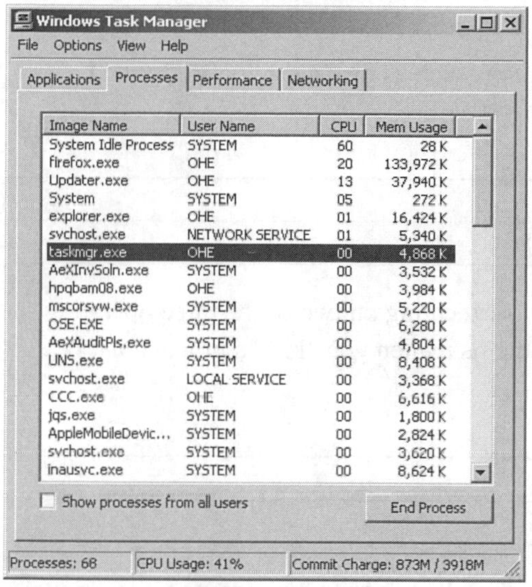

FIGURE 1-19 Task Manager Utility in Windows XP

Exercise 1.6.7

Open the Task Manager in Windows. What type of information about the computer is available? How would this be useful for monitoring your system?

_____

_____

_____

Exercise 1.6.8

With the Task Manager open in Windows, sort the running processes by CPU cycles. What process is using the most CPU time? Sort the processes by memory. What process is using the most RAM?

_____

Exercise 1.6.9

The utilities similar to Task Manager on Linux and Mac OS X are different and showcase different information. Choose one of these alternate OS utilities and compare the information given to the Task Manager information in Windows. The Mac OS X utility is called Activity Monitor, and you can access it within the same Utilities folder as the System Profiler utility. On a Linux machine, you can get process information in real time by using the command **top**.

_____

_____

_____

_____

Lab 1.6 Review

1. Why is it important to know your system specifications such as disk capacity, RAM, and processor information?

   _____

   _____

   _____

2. Use the web to research how to stop a process that is executing on two of the three operating systems (Windows, Linux, and Mac OS). What is the risk when you "kill" a process that is running on your machine?

   _____

   _____

   _____

3. Operating system updates and firmware updates for installed devices are essential to continued functionality and security for a computer by itself or on a network. Use the web to locate where you can find current information on patches and updates for two operating systems. What is the risk associated with not updating your system? Is there a risk associated with completing the system updates? Justify your position.

   _____

   _____

   _____

   _____

Chapter 2

Introduction to Computer Networking

This chapter will allow you to practice the fundamentals of computer networking, including how to manage network connections and networked resources on a PC. The labs in this chapter are designed to reinforce concepts from Chapter 2 of your *Introduction to Networking* textbook and allow you to explore some of the more important ideas with greater depth. You will explore the different types of networks available and analyze how to add new connections to each topology as a network grows. You will also use the command-line interface on different operating systems, which will be useful for network troubleshooting in later chapters. At the end of this chapter, you should be able to

- Create a basic network connection
- Describe shared resources and connect to a shared resource on a network
- Describe the basic network types and topologies and know how to extend them to include new connections
- Access the command line on common operating systems including Windows, Mac OS, and Linux
- Use Linux man pages to explore the functionality of commands

Lab 2.1: Connecting Computers

Approximate Lab Time: 15–20 min.

Materials Needed: Paper/Pencil, PC Lab (Windows), Textbook, and Internet Research

This lab reviews the fundamentals of network connections, the means of connecting two or more computers or electronic devices to each other. You will review the foundations of networking and then explore how to create a peer-to-peer network and establish a new network connection on your PC. Compile a lab report of the solutions to the assigned exercises and include a review of the work necessary to arrive at the solution.

Networking Foundations

A network is formed when any two or more devices are connected and allowed to share information (even if it only occurs in one direction). There are several key things that you need to establish a network:

- **Media:** This is the physical structure on which the signal will transmit (in wireless networks, this is the open air).
- **Interface:** This is the means by which the computer can access the media.
- **Signal:** This is the means of transmission of information, such as electrical signals on copper wire.
- **Pattern:** This is the established format for the signals to be interpreted by the computing device; a protocol is a more complex pattern that houses the individual bit patterns.
- **Timing:** This is the established synchronization between the communicating devices so that each knows precisely when a pattern starts and ends.

Exercise 2.1.1

Explain why all of these elements are necessary for allowing one device to communicate with another. What happens if one of them is not present? Explain this circumstance for all five elements.

_____

_____

_____

_____

_____

_____

_____

Exercise 2.1.2

Most modern computers have device drivers for network interfaces that manage most of these elements automatically. What characteristics of modern computer networks allow this type of integration? Use your textbook and Internet research to support your answer.

_____

_____

_____

_____

Peer-to-Peer Networks

Peer-to-peer networks are the simplest type of network. There is no infrastructure involved with their creation or use. The devices act as equals on the network to communicate back and forth with a pre-decided protocol.

Exercise 2.1.3

For this exercise, you will enable peer-to-peer communication on your Windows XP machine. Complete the steps that follow to enable this service. What other networking services are available for installation?

_____

_____

_____

STEP 1.   Open the Control Panel on your XP machine. From the **Start** menu, choose **Settings** and then choose **Control Panel**.

STEP 2.   Choose **Add or Remove Programs** from the Control Panel options that appear. The result should be similar to what is shown in Figure 2-1.

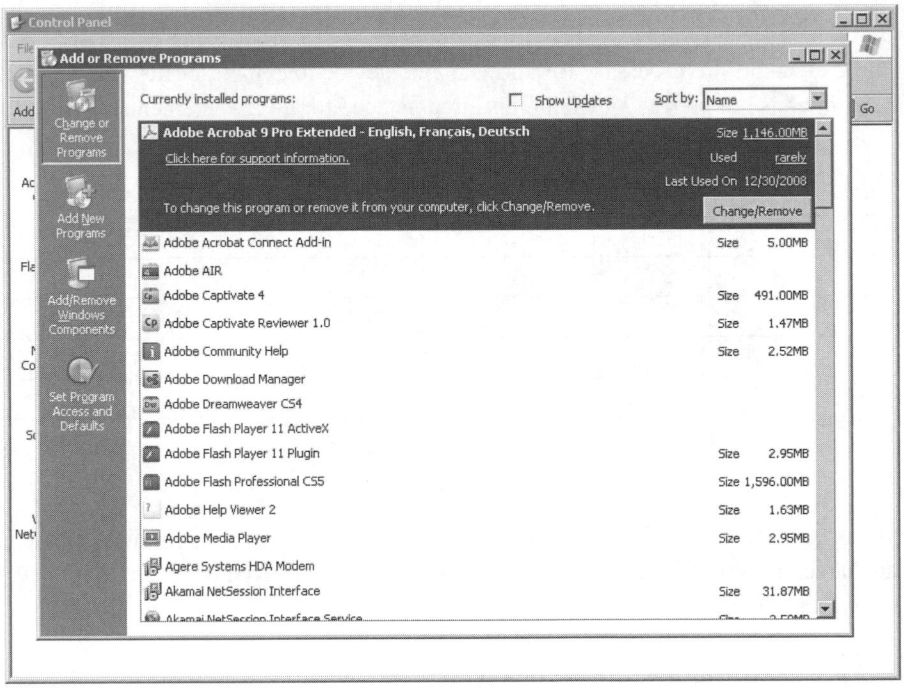

FIGURE 2-1   Add or Remove Programs Menu in Windows XP

STEP 3.   Choose **Add/Remove Windows Components**; this will open a new window, the Windows Components Wizard. You can see an example of this in Figure 2-2.

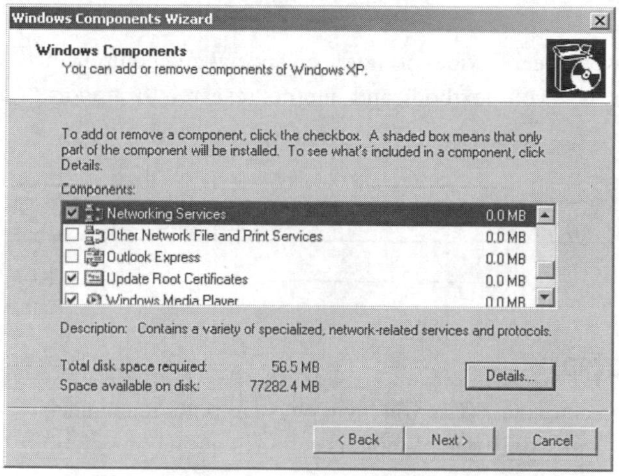

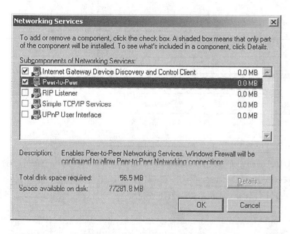

FIGURE 2-2   Windows Components Wizard in Windows XP

STEP 4.   Click the **Networking Services** entry and click the **Details** button. This will open a new window, Networking Services, like the one shown in Figure 2-3.

FIGURE 2-3   Networking Services in Windows XP

STEP 5.   Select the check box next to **Peer-to-Peer** and click **OK**.

If you are creating a wired connection (such as an RJ-45 Ethernet connection) between two PCs, you need a special type of cable called a crossover cable to complete the connection. The PC interface on both ends is designed to connect to a switched device, so its input and output lines need to be reversed to connect to a device with the same type of network interface as itself (such as another host or a router). This aligns the output lines to the input lines of the other PC and vice versa.

Exercise 2.1.4

Briefly explain why wireless connections between peer devices do not need specialized equipment like a crossover cable to connect to each other. Use your textbook and Internet research to support your answer.

_____

_____

_____

Creating a Network Connection

You can establish as many network connections on your PC as you have physical ports to connect (this is true of routing devices as well), but typically only one of them is active at a time by default. For example, if you have a wireless connection and a wired connection, only one will be used to send and retrieve the information that appears in your web browser. The steps that follow guide you through the process of establishing a new network connection on your PC or virtual machine.

Exercise 2.1.5

For this exercise, you will be creating a new network connection on your Windows PC. List the types of connections that are available to choose. Record the settings that you choose in each step.

_____

_____

_____

> **NOTE:** Depending on the setup of your PC lab, you might already be connected to the Internet or an Internet-enabled network. If you are connected, you should not click the final Finish button if you select the Internet option or you might have duplicate connections.

STEP 1.   Open the **Control Panel** and select **Network Connections**. You will see a window similar to what is shown in Figure 2-4.

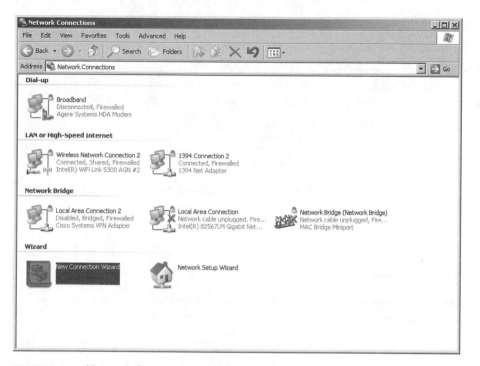

FIGURE 2-4   Network Connections in Windows XP

STEP 2.   From this folder, open the New Connection Wizard. When the window opens, click **Next**. The window you will see should look similar to Figure 2-5.

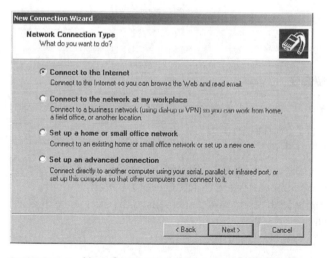

FIGURE 2-5   New Connection Wizard in Windows XP

STEP 3.   For this exercise, you will be establishing an advanced connection to allow other computers to connect to your machine. Choose **Set up an advanced connection** and click the **Next** button.

STEP 4. Choose **Accept incoming connections** and click **Next**.

STEP 5. Choose a device on which to allow incoming connections.

STEP 6. Click **Next** on each page until you are presented with the Networking Software page of the wizard. Choose the services you would like to have enabled, and then click **Next**. List the Networking Software options with which you are presented, and then click **Next**.

STEP 7. Click **Finish** to complete the wizard.

Lab 2.1 Review

1. Explain the difference between a network device and a peripheral device and give examples of each. You can use your textbook and the Internet to research your answer.

   _____

   _____

   _____

2. Explain why you would want to limit the type of incoming connections that you allow on a computer. Use your textbook and Internet research to support your answer.

   _____

   _____

   _____

3. Explain the purpose and benefits of a peer-to-peer network.

   _____

   _____

   _____

Lab 2.2: Network Drives

Approximate Lab Time: 30–40 min.

Materials Needed: Paper/Pencil, PC Lab (Windows)

In small offices or businesses, it is often more cost effective and efficient to have a shared resource than to provide that resource to every person or computer in the office. One of the most common examples of this is a networked printer. Compile a lab report of the solutions to the assigned exercises and include a review of the work necessary to arrive at the solution.

Shared Resources

Using networks allows more than just the exchange of information between two client computers. Consider, for example, the cost of providing a printer to each client machine in an organization. If you instead just buy one printer that can be shared across the office over the local network, how much money will the organization save?

Exercise 2.2.1

If an organization has 30 users, each with his or her own PC, what is the comparative cost of buying a $120 printer for each user versus the cost of buying a single, higher-capacity $500 printer that can be used by the entire office? What is the drawback to having only a single printer? What is the cost of having two additional backup printers for the office compared to having individual printers? How many shared printers can be purchased and still be less expensive than individual printers?

_____

_____

_____

Networking a resource also allows you to maximize its use. In the printer example, not everyone will be printing constantly, so there will be long periods of time when each printer is idle. If the resource is shared, you maximize its use. This same scenario is true of shared storage devices and shared services.

Exercise 2.2.2

If each of the 30 users in an organization prints an average of 22 pages per hour and a shared printer has the capacity to print 180 pages per hour, how many shared printers will be needed to prevent overloading each printer's capacity? Would there be a benefit to having more than the exact number needed? Justify your answer.

_____

_____

_____

Mapping a Network Drive

In most organizations, it is more effective to have a centralized storage server for saving files and resources. This type of centralization allows easier file management for the administrators and allows client (or user) computers to be swapped easily without the need for significant data transfers or loss of information. The following steps guide you through the process of mapping a network drive on your Windows PC or virtual machine.

> **NOTE:** Centralized storage on a server makes use of a single (or multiple) high-storage–capacity drives that are more efficient than providing individual storage on user machines. This system also allows easier backup of the mission-critical information that an organization possesses. The client machines in this case simply have access to the network resource.

Exercise 2.2.3

In this exercise, you will map a network location to your local machine. Record the steps that you follow for the process, and record the network location that is mapped to the letter you choose.

_____

_____

_____

STEP 1.   Open the My Computer icon on your desktop (or whatever the computer has been named). From the window that opens, select the Tools menu and choose **Map Network Drive**. You should see a view similar to Figure 2-6.

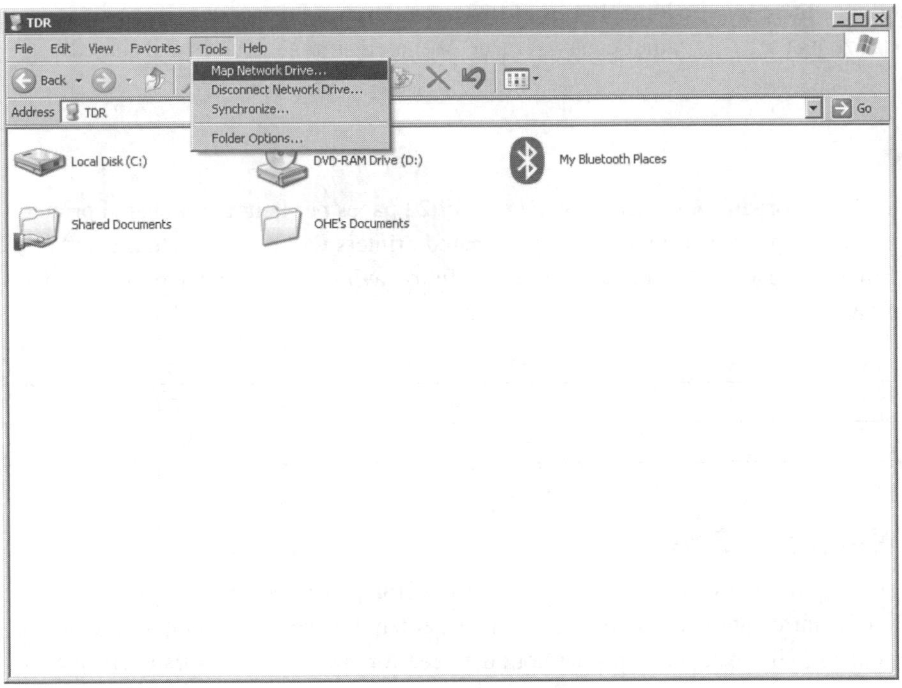

FIGURE 2-6   Mapping a Network Drive in Windows XP

STEP 2.   The Map Network Drive window appears. There are two entries to complete on this screen. You should select an unused drive letter and a network location for these fields. You can see an example of this screen in Figure 2-7.

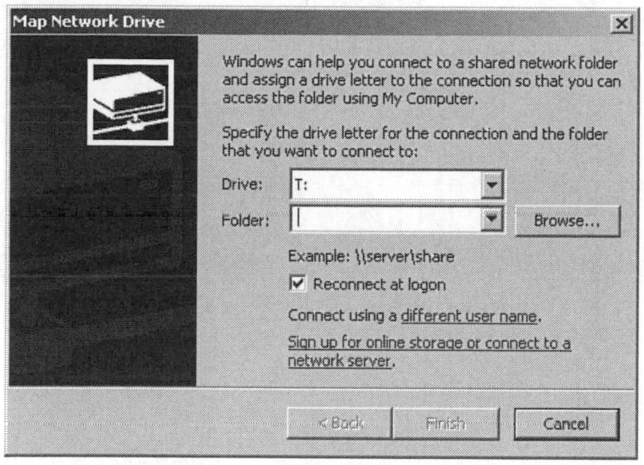

FIGURE 2-7 Map Network Drive Window

STEP 3. If you click the **Browse** button, you will be shown the available network folders from your device on the local network. If you do not have a network enabled, you can still complete the exercise by mapping a local folder.

STEP 4. Choose whether you want to reconnect at login by selecting or deselecting the check box. Click **Finish** when you are done, and the new drive letter will appear in the My Computer folder.

Exercise 2.2.4

What are the drawbacks of using a networked drive for storing important documents? Use your textbook and the Internet to support your conclusion.

_____

_____

_____

Creating a Shortcut to a Network Resource

Some network resources are used frequently, so it is helpful to establish a quick connection to them on your machine. For a Windows machine, you can create a link to a web-based resource on your desktop.

Exercise 2.2.5

For this exercise, you will create a link to a web resource on your desktop. You should record the address of the link that you create.

_____

STEP 1. Open a web browser (such as Internet Explorer) to the address for which you want to create a shortcut. Copy the Uniform Resource Locator (URL) from the address bar.

STEP 2. On the desktop, right-click in an empty area, select **New**, and then choose **Shortcut**. This will open a new dialog window, Create Shortcut. You can see an example of this in Figure 2-8.

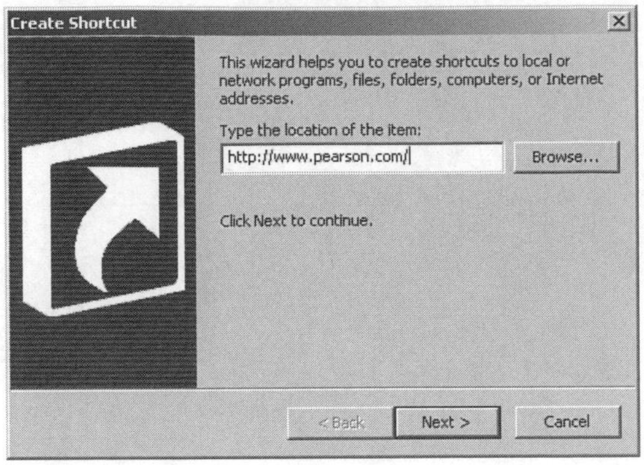

Create Shortcut   ⊠

This wizard helps you to create shortcuts to local or network programs, files, folders, computers, or Internet addresses.

Type the location of the item:

| http://www.pearson.com/ | Browse... |

Click Next to continue.

| < Back | Next > | Cancel |

FIGURE 2-8   Create Shortcut Window

STEP 3.   Paste the URL from the web browser into the location text box. Click **Next**.

STEP 4.   On the next screen, enter the name you want to be displayed for the shortcut; then click **Finish**. This will create a shortcut icon for the resource on your desktop. You can see an example of this in Figure 2-9.

FIGURE 2-9   Shortcut Example

Exercise 2.2.6

How often should you verify that the network resource is connected correctly? What will happen to your connection if the web-based resource gets moved or taken offline? Justify your conclusions.

_____

_____

_____

Lab 2.2 Review

1. Why is it infeasible to create a shortcut to every web-based resource (such as a website) that you use frequently? What is a better alternative to creating shortcuts on your desktop for frequently visited sites?

_____

_____

_____

_____

_____

2. Should you create multiple mounted drives for different folders on the same network computer? What will this accomplish, and why is it a good or bad idea? Justify your conclusion with support from your textbook or Internet research.

_____

_____

_____

3. The two primary functions of a network are sharing resources and communicating between devices. Why is the ability to share resources advantageous in a network? What benefit does it provide?

_____

_____

_____

Lab 2.3: Network Types and Topologies

Approximate Lab Time: 25–30 min.

Materials Needed: Paper/Pencil, Textbook, and Internet Research

In this lab, you will analyze the various types and topologies of networks that can be created for interlinking computing devices. As part of this lab, you will explore what it would take to add a new device to each kind of common network topology and determine the upper limit of adding new devices based on network resource limitations. Compile a lab report of the solutions to the assigned exercises and include a review of the work necessary to arrive at the solution.

Network Types

There are a number of ways to classify networks. This includes the number of nodes in a network, the arrangement of nodes in a network, and the geographical distance covered by the network. The description used for the network can change depending upon the information you are seeking. For example, a network can have a bus topology and be a LAN with 20 nodes all at the same time.

Exercise 2.3.1

Briefly define LAN, MAN, PAN, and WAN. What is the critical distinction for these networks? What is the classification metric used here?

_____

_____

_____

_____

_____

_____

Exercise 2.3.2

Briefly define the term *network topology*. What is the metric used to define networks by topology?

_____

_____

_____

Network Topologies

Network topologies are often defined by the logical organization of the interconnected devices, despite the physical arrangement of them. The choice of network topology is often dependent upon the type of network to be created, the number of devices to connect, and the cost of the network. The metrics for evaluating networks are the number of nodes, the number of links, and the number of messages that must be passed to transmit information. Consider the following topologies as you complete the exercises.

Ring

This is an older topology that connects devices in sequence in a circular pattern. Transmission is in one direction, so any message that must travel in the opposite direction must traverse the entire ring. You can see an example of this topology in Figure 2-10. Newer versions of this topology are still in use today, where double-ring topologies allow communication in both directions. This is also used as a logical topology because it can outperform a bus (the underlying physical topology in this case is typically a star).

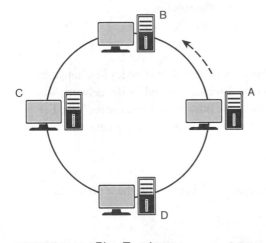

FIGURE 2-10 Ring Topology

Exercise 2.3.3

Using the ring topology shown in Figure 2-10, how many actual messages would it take (the number of hops on the network) to send a message from A to B? How many actual messages would it take to send a message from B to A? How many additional links would be required to add a new node E between C and D? How would this affect the number of messages it takes to traverse the ring?

_____

_____

_____

Bus

In a bus topology, devices are split off from a central line. The devices share the central line and all devices receive all messages. A terminator is required to prevent messages from bouncing back onto the line after being transmitted. You can see an example of a bus topology in Figure 2-11.

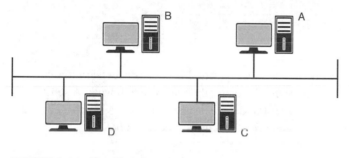

FIGURE 2-11   Bus Topology

Exercise 2.3.4

Using the bus topology from Figure 2-11, how many actual messages would it take to send a message from A to D? How many actual messages would it take to send a message from D to A? How many additional links would be required to add a new node E between C and B? How would the added node affect the network?

_____

_____

_____

Star

A star network uses either a hub or switch in the center, and each device has a single connection to the central routing device. With a hub, all traffic is forwarded to all other connections. With a switch, it is sent only to the specific destination. Figure 2-12 shows an example of a star network topology.

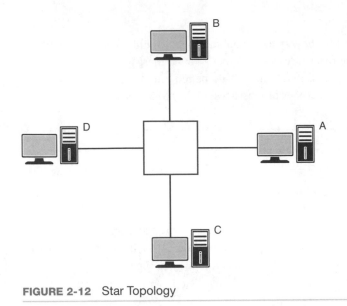

FIGURE 2-12   Star Topology

Exercise 2.3.5

Using the star topology in Figure 2-12, consider the number of actual messages necessary to send a message from A to B. How many messages are sent if the central device is a hub when A sends a message to B? How many messages are sent if the central device is a switch when A sends a message to B? What effect does adding a new node E between C and D have on the network?

_____

_____

_____

_____

_____

_____

_____

_____

Mesh

A mesh network interconnects every device in the network to every other device in the network. This allows redundant links in case of problems but requires more overhead in cabling. An example of a mesh topology is shown in Figure 2-13.

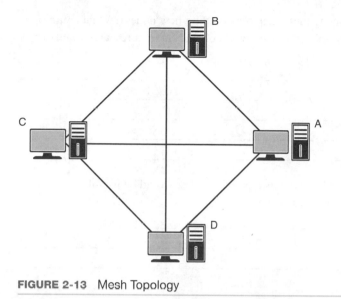

FIGURE 2-13 Mesh Topology

Exercise 2.3.6

Using the mesh topology shown in Figure 2-13, how many actual messages are necessary to send a message from A to D? How many actual messages are needed to send a message from A to B? How many links would be required to add a new node E between C and D? How many links would be required to add a new node F if E is already added?

_____

_____

_____

_____

_____

_____

Lab 2.3 Review

1. What are some devices that you can connect to a PAN? You can use your textbook and Internet research to support your answer.

_____

_____

_____

2. Of the network topologies covered in this lab, which of them have a single point of failure for the network? A single point of failure is where one device or connection going down will stop all network traffic. Justify your position.

_____

_____

_____

3. What are the limiting factors for growing mesh networks (adding new nodes)? What are the limiting factors for growing star networks? Use your textbook and Internet research to justify your answer.

_____

_____

_____

_____

_____

4. Give an example of a MAN and describe why this type of network would be useful. Use your textbook and Internet research to justify your answer.

_____

_____

_____

Lab 2.4: Command-Line Interface

Approximate Lab Time: 10–15 min.
Materials Needed: Paper/Pencil, PC Lab (Windows, Mac OS, and/or Linux)

Some network devices do not have a convenient graphical user interface (GUI) for you to explore their settings visually, so you must access them through a command-line interface. Modern devices often have either a web interface or command-line interface for accessing and changing their settings, where the command-line interface can offer a more robust set of functionality than the web interface. Using the command line is also an efficient way to determine and change the settings on computers that do have a GUI. The ability to quickly navigate and use the command line on your computer will be helpful in network analysis and troubleshooting in the upcoming chapters. Compile a lab report of the solutions to the assigned exercises and include a review of the work necessary to arrive at the solution.

Networking from the Command Line

For this lab, you will be using the command-line interface on various operating systems to access network information. The command you will use is **ipconfig** (or **ifconfig** on Mac OS and Linux); this command returns information on the current network settings. While you might not understand all the information it provides at this point, it is important for you to be able to access the command line and get the information to return from the use of this command.

> **NOTE:** You can also use the command line to determine information across multiple devices by accessing them through the command line of your own computer through remote connections.

Exercise 2.4.1

For this exercise, you will follow the instructions for Windows, Mac OS, and Linux (or whatever subset of these operating systems is available to you in the lab). Record the steps that you take, and copy the output from the command into your lab report.

_____

_____

_____

_____

_____

_____

_____

_____

_____

_____

_____

_____

_____

_____

_____

_____

_____

_____

_____

Windows Command Line

To access the command line in Windows XP, follow these steps:

STEP 1. Select the **Start** menu and choose the **Run** option.

STEP 2. In the text box that appears, type **cmd** (for the command interface). A new command window should appear, similar to Figure 2-14.

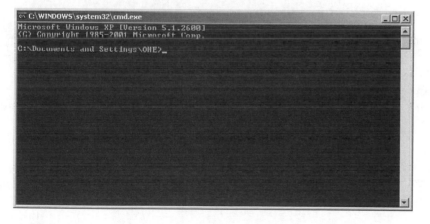

FIGURE 2-14 Command Window

To execute the **ipconfig** command and copy the results to the system Clipboard for pasting, follow these steps:

STEP 1.   In the command window at the > prompt (where the flashing cursor appears), type **ipconfig** and press the **Enter** key.

STEP 2.   Right-click in the results window and choose **Select All**.

STEP 3.   Press the **Enter** key to copy the results (which can then be pasted in a Word or Notepad document).

Mac OS Command Line

To access the Mac OS command-line interface, follow these steps:

STEP 1.   Open the **MacintoshHD** folder and open the **Utilities** subfolder.

STEP 2.   Double-click the Terminal icon in the **Utilities** folder. A new window will appear where you can type commands.

> **NOTE:** Mac OS X typically follows the Linux syntax for the command-line interface as opposed to the Windows syntax.

To execute the **ifconfig** command and copy the results, follow these steps:

STEP 1.   In the command window at the > prompt, type **ifconfig** and press **Enter**.

STEP 2.   Use the mouse to select the results you want to copy, right-click the mouse, and choose **Copy**. The results can now be pasted into a word processing or text document.

Linux Command Line

To access the command-line interface in a Fedora Linux environment, follow these steps:

STEP 1.   Open the **Applications** menu and select the **System Tools** entry. You can see an example of this in Figure 2-15.

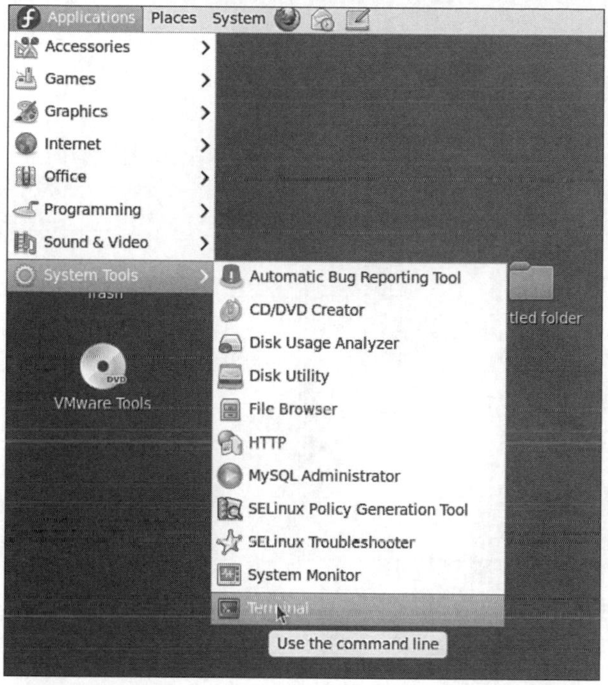

FIGURE 2-15   Applications View in Fedora Linux

STEP 2.   Click the Terminal icon to launch a new terminal window.

> **NOTE:** The steps given here are for the Fedora Linux OS. The variety of Linux versions makes this process somewhat different for each incarnation, but the commands are common to all implementations of Linux. When you access the Terminal, it is worth dragging it to the desktop or the taskbar to create a direct shortcut to it for later use.

To enter the **ifconfig** command and copy the results, follow these steps:

STEP 1.   In the command window, enter the **ifconfig** command at the > prompt. You can see an example of this in Figure 2-16.

```
┌────────────────────────────────────────────────────────────────┐
│ □              Student1@localhost:~              [_][□][x]        │
├────────────────────────────────────────────────────────────────┤
│ File  Edit  View  Terminal  Help                                 │
│ [Student1@localhost ~]$ ifconfig                                 │
│ eth10     Link encap:Ethernet  HWaddr 00:0C:29:79:43:3C          │
│           inet addr:10.251.209.106  Bcast:10.251.209.255  Mask:255.255.255.0 │
│           inet6 addr: fe80::20c:29ff:fe79:433c/64 Scope:Link     │
│           UP BROADCAST RUNNING MULTICAST  MTU:1500  Metric:1      │
│           RX packets:86580 errors:0 dropped:0 overruns:0 frame:0  │
│           TX packets:46531 errors:0 dropped:0 overruns:0 carrier:0│
│           collisions:0 txqueuelen:1000                           │
│           RX bytes:119738241 (114.1 MiB)  TX bytes:3328848 (3.1 MiB) │
│           Interrupt:19 Base address:0x2000                       │
│                                                                  │
│ lo        Link encap:Local Loopback                              │
│           inet addr:127.0.0.1  Mask:255.0.0.0                    │
│           inet6 addr: ::1/128 Scope:Host                         │
│           UP LOOPBACK RUNNING  MTU:16436  Metric:1               │
│           RX packets:15 errors:0 dropped:0 overruns:0 frame:0    │
│           TX packets:15 errors:0 dropped:0 overruns:0 carrier:0  │
│           collisions:0 txqueuelen:0                              │
│           RX bytes:1056 (1.0 KiB)  TX bytes:1056 (1.0 KiB)       │
│                                                                  │
│ [Student1@localhost ~]$ ▐                                        │
│                                                                  │
└────────────────────────────────────────────────────────────────┘
```

FIGURE 2-16   Terminal Window in Fedora Linux

STEP 2.   Use the mouse to select the results, right-click, and choose **Copy**. The text can now be pasted into a word processing or text document.

Lab 2.4 Review

1. Compare the output of two of the operating systems in which you entered the **ipconfig** or **ifconfig** command. What common information was given by the operating systems?

_____

_____

_____

_____

2. Outside of networking, is there a benefit to knowing how to access the command-line interface of an operating system? Use your textbook and Internet research to support your answer.

_____

_____

3. Windows and Mac OS focus more on the graphical user interface of the operating system instead of the command-line interface. Why has this focus been selected, and what marketing advantage is there to this emphasis? Use your textbook and Internet research to support your answer.

_____

_____

_____

_____

Lab 2.5: Linux man Pages

Approximate Lab Time: 10–15 min.
Prerequisite: Lab 2.4

Materials Needed: Paper/Pencil, PC Lab (Linux)

Linux man pages are the equivalent of help files for the commands available on the Linux command-line interface. These pages provide details on how to use the command and what options are available for it. This is an excellent way to gather information on a command with which you are unfamiliar. Compile a lab report of the solutions to the assigned exercises and include a review of the work necessary to arrive at the solution.

Using man Pages

The Linux man pages (short for manual pages) are accessed from the Terminal (the command-line interface). The **man** command is executed by typing **man** followed by a space and the command for which you want the help information.

> **NOTE:** You can also view Linux man pages in a web browser online at www.linuxmanpages.com.

Exercise 2.5.1

For this exercise, you will use the man page for the **man** command to get more information on man pages. To complete this, type **man man** in the Terminal window at the > prompt. From the information given in the man page for the man command, what is the purpose of a man page and why are they useful?

_____

_____

_____

The man Page Structure

For this lab, you will be running the **man man** command again to gather information for the following exercises.

Exercise 2.5.2

What are the sections contained in a man page?

_____

_____

Exercise 2.5.3

What are four of the available options for use with the **man** command?

_____

_____

_____

_____

_____

Lab 2.5 Review

1. According to the man page for ifconfig, what is the purpose of the **ifconfig** command and what information does it return by default?

   _____

   _____

   _____

   _____

2. List three of the command-line options available for the **ifconfig** command. You can get this information directly from the man page.

   _____

   _____

   _____

3. What information is returned when you enter the following commands in Linux?

   ```
   man -f ifconfig
   man -w ifconfig
   ```

   _____

   _____

   _____

Chapter 3

Building TCP/IP Networks

This chapter will allow you to explore the common models of networking from the physical media connection to the application that displays the information, including how these layers interact and how they map to real networking devices. The labs in this chapter are designed to reinforce concepts from Chapter 3 of your *Introduction to Networking* textbook and allow you to explore some of the more important ideas with greater depth. You will explore the different types of network reference models available and analyze how each one applies to real network technology. You will also use packet capturing to look at real network traffic and explore the data link layer of networking. At the end of this chapter, you should be able to

- Explain the purpose of network reference models
- Describe the layers of the OSI reference model and explain what each layer provides
- Describe the layers of the TCP/IP model and relate it to the OSI model and real networking equipment
- Capture live packet information on a network and explain the data link layer portion of the packets captured
- Enable network resources such as shared printers and file sharing on your own PC

Lab 3.1: Network Reference Models

Approximate Lab Time: 10–15 min.

Materials Needed: Paper/Pencil, Textbook, and Internet Research

This lab reviews the importance of modeling communication on a network. This will include a review of the state of networking before standardized reference models existed and the impact that they have on interoperability. Compile a lab report of the solutions to the assigned exercises and include a review of the work necessary to arrive at the solution.

The Purpose of Reference Models

Before the use of reference models for network communication, all the vendors of interoperable equipment worked in proprietary realms, and it was impossible to feasibly connect the devices from two different vendors together.

Exercise 3.1.1

What would happen if wireless devices were not governed by the Wi-Fi Alliance and each vendor had its own standards and protocols? What impact would this have on your personal life or business communications?

_____

_____

_____

_____

_____

Reference models provide more than just a means of standardization. They also provide a way to visualize and describe communication, even if we cannot physically see or observe the connection itself.

Exercise 3.1.2

Give another example of a model that is used to visualize something that is difficult to observe or perceive. How does the model make it easier to understand?

_____

_____

_____

_____

Modeling Communication

When dealing with networking reference models, the model is divided into layers of communication. These layers are designed so that the layer below encapsulates the structure from the layer above and serves it to the layer below. This is true of both of the models you will explore in the labs of this chapter: the Open Systems Interconnection (OSI) model and the TCP/IP model.

Both of these models look at communication from the bottom layer of the physical connection between devices (including radio frequencies over air for wireless connections) all the way to the top layers of the software application that invokes the communication.

Exercise 3.1.3

Based on what you already know about networks, what are the different layers you think would be necessary for communication to be mapped to a model? Consider direct connections between host devices and connections that require other routing equipment, such as a hub, switch, or router.

_____

_____

_____

Exercise 3.1.4

The granularity of the reference model will often determine the usefulness of the model. What will happen if a model is too general? What will happen if a model is too granular (too focused on individual detail)?

_____

_____

_____

Lab 3.1 Review

1. Why would a three-layer model of communication that has the layers physical, network, and application be insufficient to adequately describe network communication?

_____

_____

_____

_____

_____

2. What is the history of the OSI reference model? How did it come about and why was it created? Use your textbook and Internet research to support your answer.

_____

_____

_____

_____

_____

3. What is the history of the TCP/IP model? Why was it created? Use your textbook and Internet research to support your answer.

_____

_____

_____

_____

Lab 3.2: The OSI Reference Model

Approximate Lab Time: 20–25 min.
Prerequisite: Lab 3.1

Materials Needed: Paper/Pencil, Textbook, and Internet Research

This lab reviews the fundamentals of the OSI reference model, the visualization of the layers over which communications between devices can occur. You will review the model in general and then examine how it relates to routing and host-to-host connections. Compile a lab report of the solutions to the assigned exercises and include a review of the work necessary to arrive at the solution.

The OSI Reference Model

The OSI reference model gave a common language to networking. It allowed the different stages of communication on a network to be visualized and standardized. You can see the layers of the OSI model in Figure 3-1.

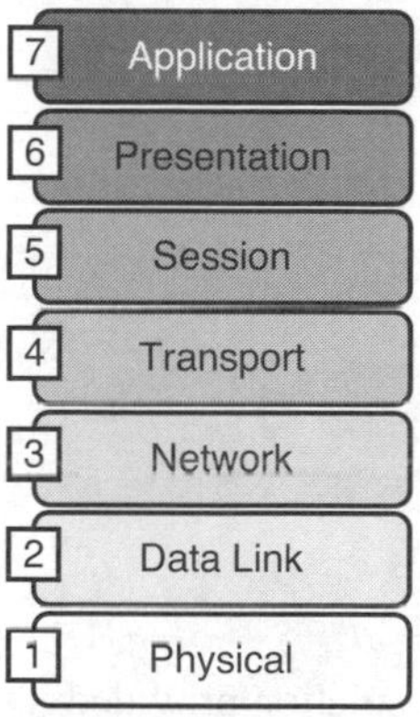

FIGURE 3-1   OSI Reference Model

Exercise 3.2.1

Using Figure 3-1, define each layer of the OSI model in your own words and state what each layer provides. Use your textbook or Internet research to support your answer.

_____

_____

_____

_____

_____

_____

_____

_____

_____

_____

_____

_____

_____

Comparing the OSI Model Layers to Functionality

Using the principle of the OSI model that each layer encapsulates the information from the layer above it and serves it to the layer below it, consider the encapsulation diagram in Figure 3-2. The layers of the model provide the means of translating the data from the application layer into a routable frame that is converted into physical bits transmitted by the physical layer.

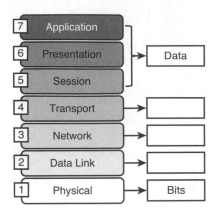

FIGURE 3-2   Data Representation in the OSI Model

Exercise 3.2.2

Using Figure 3-2 as a basis, complete the diagram to show the intermediate encapsulation provided by each layer. Use your textbook and Internet research to support your answer.

Using the OSI Model in Network Communication

Consider a host-to-host communication over a network (such as a peer-to-peer network) where the transmission of information is initiated by a network-aware application. You can see a diagram of this communication in Figure 3-3. The data that is transmitted from a device must be deencapsulated when it is received for the data to be usable by the recipient application.

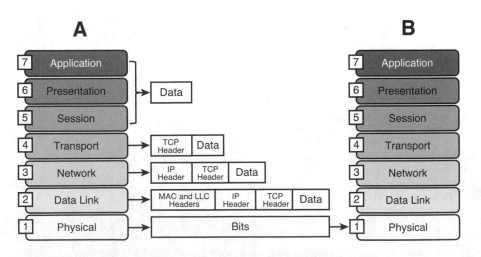

FIGURE 3-3   Host-to-Host Communication Using the OSI Model

Exercise 3.2.3

Briefly explain the deencapsulation steps in the communication from host B receiving a message from host A destined for an active application.

_____

_____

_____

_____

Exercise 3.2.4

Explain why routing devices do not need the upper layers of the OSI model to route traffic. What is the highest layer of the OSI model used by the router to decide where to forward traffic?

_____

_____

_____

_____

Lab 3.2 Review

1. How does the abstraction of the physical layer facilitate interoperability across networks using different types of physical wires?

_____

_____

_____

_____

2. The OSI model is not directly implemented in networking and often the distinction between the layers will blur in implementation. Why does it endure despite these issues? Use your textbook and Internet research to justify your answer.

_____

_____

_____

3. Given the purpose of each, is it necessary to retain the top three layers of the OSI model as separate entities? Use the textbook and Internet research to justify your answer.

_____

_____

Lab 3.3: The TCP/IP Model

Approximate Lab Time: 10–15 min.
Prerequisite: Lab 3.2
Materials Needed: Paper/Pencil, Textbook, and Internet Research

This lab reviews the fundamentals of the TCP/IP reference model, another visualization of the layers over which communications between devices can occur. You will review the model in general and then examine how it relates to the OSI model and common protocols used at each layer. Compile a lab report of the solutions to the assigned exercises and include a review of the work necessary to arrive at the solution.

The TCP/IP Network Model

Transport Control Protocol/Internet Protocol (TCP/IP) is an enduring set of protocols with diverse applications that was developed by the Department of Defense with its work on ARPANET, which evolved to become the Internet you use today. The TCP/IP protocol suite is based on a networking reference model constructed by the Department of Defense. This model of networking is considered more direct, but the lack of granularity has caused the OSI model to endure.

Exercise 3.3.1

Using your textbook and Internet research, create a mapping between the TCP/IP model and the OSI reference model. What are the distinct differences between them?

_____

_____

_____

_____

_____

TCP/IP Model Protocols and Functions

The TCP/IP protocol suite has endured from its early days on ARPANET to what is now known as the Internet protocol suite. The common protocols that comprise this suite are shown (separated by layer) in Figure 3-4.

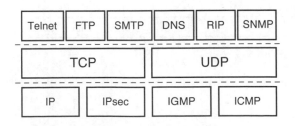

FIGURE 3-4 Common TCP/IP Protocols

Exercise 3.3.2

Identify the layer in which each protocol resides according to the TCP/IP model.

_____

_____

_____

_____

_____

Exercise 3.3.3

The most common protocols used from this suite are IP, TCP, and UDP. Briefly describe the purpose and function of each of these. Use your textbook and Internet research to support your answer.

_____

_____

_____

_____

_____

_____

_____

_____

Lab 3.3 Review

1. UDP is a connectionless protocol, unlike TCP, so there is no feedback on whether a packet was received. When would this type of protocol be useful and what is the benefit of using it? Use your textbook and Internet research to draw your conclusions.

   _____

   _____

   _____

   _____

2. HTTP is the common protocol used to retrieve web resources in a web browser. This runs over TCP/IP networks using TCP. What characteristics of TCP make its use in this situation desirable? Use your textbook and Internet research to draw your conclusions.

   _____

   _____

   _____

Lab 3.4: Data-Link Connections

Approximate Lab Time: 20–25 min.

Materials Needed: Paper/Pencil, PC Lab with Wireshark, Textbook, and Internet Research

This lab reviews the fundamentals of data link layer connections. You will review the structure of frames in general and then view live network traffic to see examples of how these frames operate. Compile a lab report of the solutions to the assigned exercises and include a review of the work necessary to arrive at the solution.

The Data Link Layer

The data link layer (from the OSI model) consists of frames, the most encapsulated grouping of data transmitted on a network. Unlike higher-level protocols like IP and TCP, the frames are common to the local network only and must be swapped out for new native frames as the message moves from network to network. This allows the data link layer to focus on local addressing and error correction for problems at the physical layer of the media.

Exercise 3.4.1

The data link layer introduces physical addressing in the form of Media Access Control (MAC) addresses. Each frame header in Ethernet, for example, will contain a source and destination MAC address. Why is this sufficient to route traffic locally without invoking the higher-level logical addressing? Use your textbook and Internet research to guide your conclusion.

_____

_____

_____

_____

_____

Packet Capture for Data Link Layer Connections (Wireshark)

For this lab, you will use Wireshark to capture live packet data and examine the frames that are recorded. From the captured frames, you can view the encapsulated information from the higher layers of the network communication as well.

> **NOTE:** You can download a free copy of Wireshark for your own PC from www.wireshark.org.

When you open the Wireshark program, you will be presented with the main software interface, as shown in Figure 3-5. You need to select a network interface (in the upper-left corner) for which you want to capture packets. You should choose the interface that you use to access the Internet. When you select the interface, click the Start icon next to the interface name. The packet capture should start automatically. If the packet capture does not begin, click the icon to start a new live capture in the capture window.

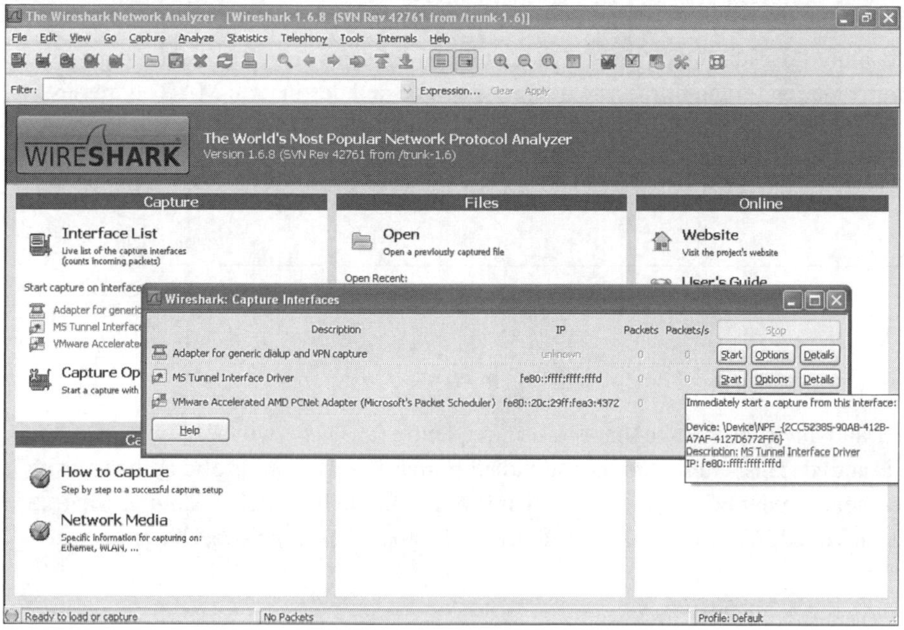

FIGURE 3-5 Wireshark Interface

Each frame that is captured will contain details at the various levels of encapsulation. Click the frame you want to review. In the area beneath the colored live capture, you will see various entries, such as Frame, Ethernet, and Internet Protocol. Clicking the + sign beside any of these will give you more information about that part of the frame. You can see this area in Figure 3-6.

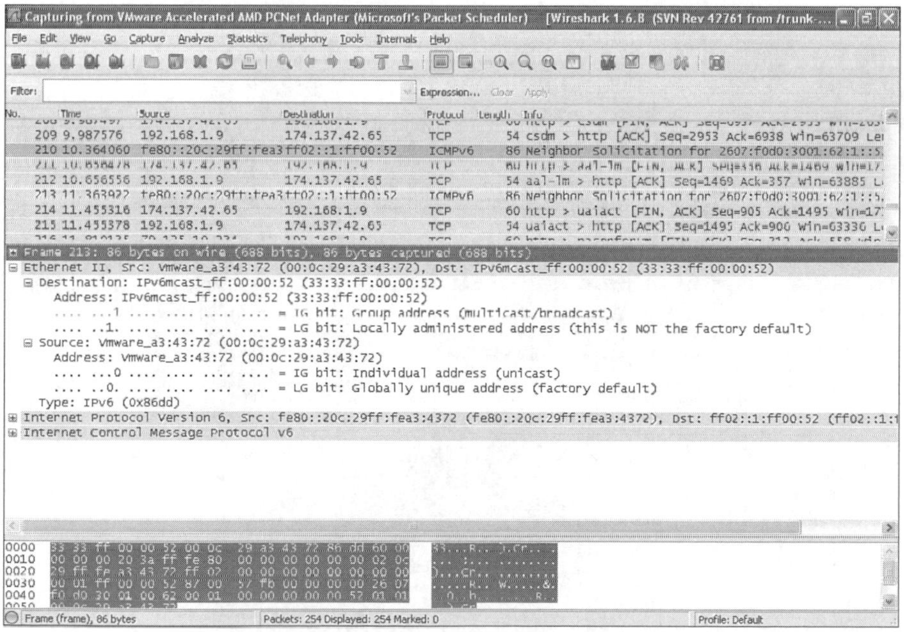

FIGURE 3-6 Wireshark Packet Capture Example

Exercise 3.4.2

Choose one of the captured packets. Click the + sign next to the Ethernet entry. This should give you the data link layer information for the frame, including the source and destination MAC addresses. Record the frame number and the source and destination MAC addresses identified by the data link layer heading. You can identify a MAC address by its format; for example, 00:26:62:65:81:07 is a MAC address. These are commonly written in hexadecimal shorthand.

_____

_____

Exercise 3.4.3

Open a web browser and navigate to a site that you use frequently (or visit www.pearson.com) while the packet capture is active. This will record the individual frames involved in resolving the website and delivering its content to your PC. When you view this traffic in the live packet capture, what protocols do you see invoked? You can find these under the Protocol heading for each frame.

_____

_____

When you stop the live packet capture, you have the option to save the captured traffic.

Packet Capture for Data Link Layer Connections (OmniPeek)

When you open OmniPeek, you should first click the New Capture icon. You can see an example of this in Figure 3-7.

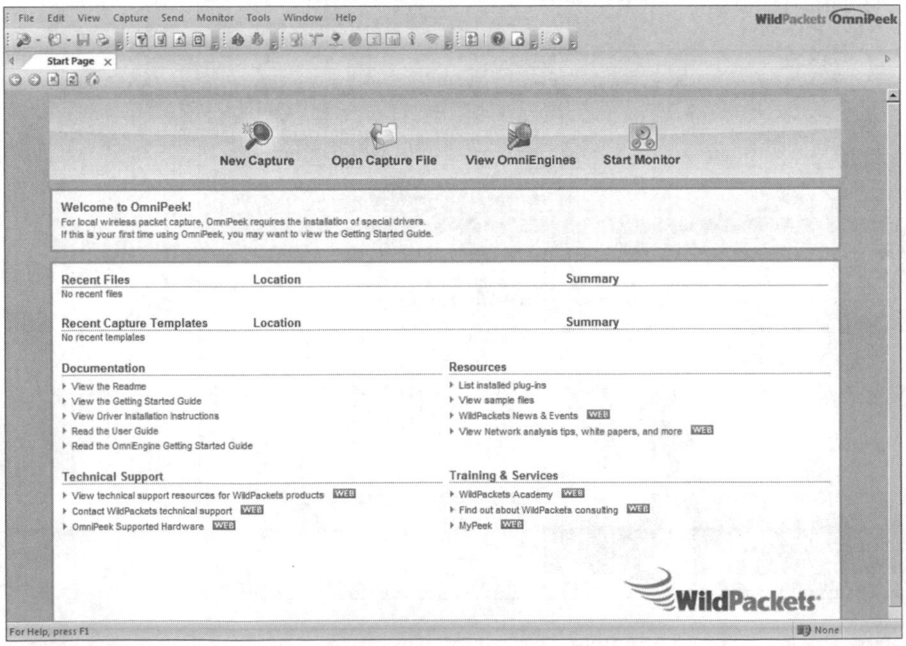

FIGURE 3-7   OmniPeek Home Screen

In the Capture Options dialog box that appears, select the network adapter (network interface) for which you would like to record traffic. You can see an example of this window in Figure 3-8. Click **OK**.

FIGURE 3-8   OmniPeek Adapter Selection

In the new capture window that appears, click the **Start Capture** button in the upper-right corner. You can see an example of the capture window in Figure 3-9.

FIGURE 3-9   OmniPeek Capture Window

Choose a packet that you want to view and double-click it to view the packet information. You can see an example of this in Figure 3-10.

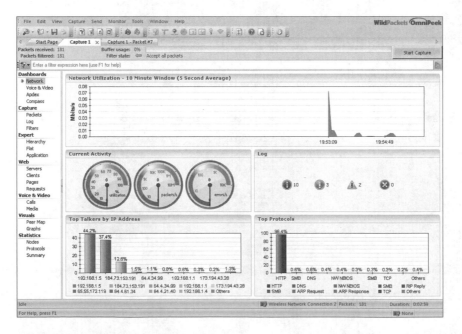

FIGURE 3-10   OmniPeek Packet View

The protocol is listed in the capture window (in a column marked Protocol) for each packet recorded.

Under Dashboards in the left-side navigation, you can select **Network** for a visual summary of the overall packet information that has been gathered. An example of this is shown in Figure 3-11.

FIGURE 3-11   OmniPeek Dashboard

Exercise 3.4.4

Choose one of the captured packets. Double-click it to open it in a new window. This should give you the data link layer information for the frame, including the source and destination MAC addresses. Record the frame number and the source and destination MAC addresses identified by the data link layer heading. You can identify a MAC address by its format; for example, 00:26:62:65:81:07 is a MAC address. These are commonly written in hexadecimal shorthand.

Exercise 3.4.5

Open a web browser and navigate to a site that you use frequently (or visit www.pearson.com) while the packet capture is active. This will record the individual frames involved in resolving the website and delivering its content to your PC. When you view this traffic in the live packet capture, what protocols do you see invoked? You can find these in the Protocol column.

Lab 3.4 Review

1. Wireshark gives you the ability to save captured traffic. This can be a great benefit to network administrators, but it can also pose a security risk. What kind of security risks does this present? Use your textbook and Internet research to support your conclusion.

2. The frame encapsulates all other information from the higher layers of the network communication. What kind of information on the network layer encapsulation is available in Wireshark?

Lab 3.5: Network Resource Configuration

Approximate Lab Time: 10–15 min.
Prerequisite: Lab 2.1

Materials Needed: Paper/Pencil, PC Lab (Windows), Textbook, and Internet Research

This lab reviews the configuration of a computer for use in a home or small office network, including the sharing of files and printers. Compile a lab report of the solutions to the assigned exercises and include a review of the work necessary to arrive at the solution.

Configuring Shared Resources

For this lab, you will configure your PC for use on a home or small office network using the Network Setup Wizard in Windows XP. To enable shared resources on your computer, complete the steps in Exercise 3.5.1.

Exercise 3.5.1

Complete the following steps to enable file and printer sharing on your Windows XP PC. Record the settings you choose. Why is it important to keep a record of this information?

_____

_____

_____

_____

STEP 1.   Open the Control Panel and choose **Network Connections**. This time, you will select the **Network Setup Wizard**.

STEP 2.   Click **Next** through the initial screens.

You might be presented with a list of disconnected hardware. In this case, you should select the check box next to **Ignore disconnected network hardware**. You can see an example of this in Figure 3-12. Click **Next** when you are finished.

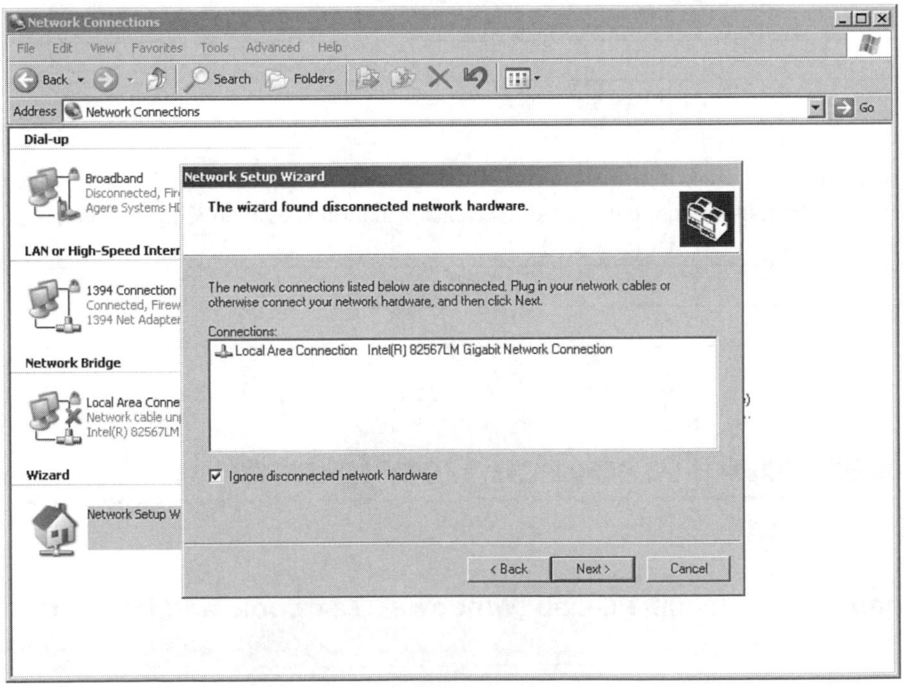

FIGURE 3-12   Disconnected Hardware Resolution

STEP 3.   The next screen asks you whether your computer is connected directly to the Internet or whether you connect through a gateway (as shown in Figure 3-13). In most cases, you will choose that you connect through a gateway (a cable modem or home router). Make your selection and click **Next**.

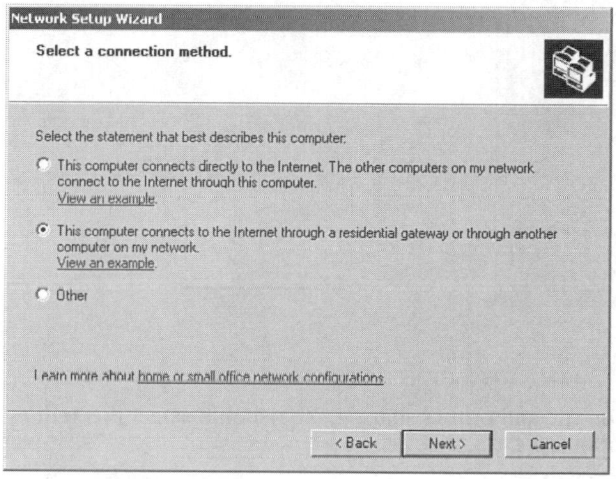

FIGURE 3-13   Gateway Settings

STEP 4.   You will then be prompted to enter a description for the computer and give the computer a name. You can see this screen in Figure 3-14. Click **Next** when you are finished.

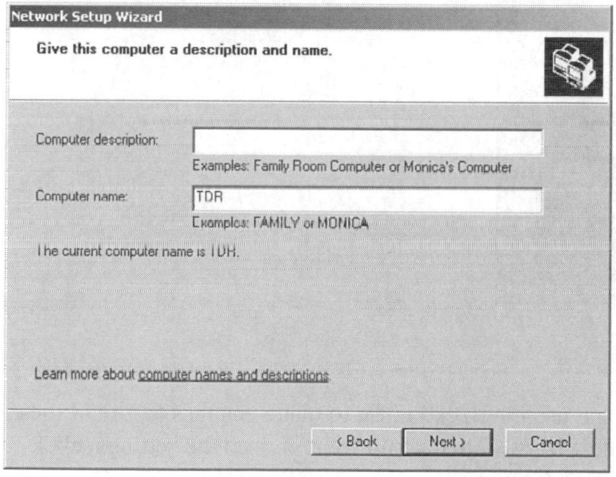

FIGURE 3-14   Computer Name and Description

STEP 5.   You will now be prompted to enter a workgroup name for the local network. You should be sure to use the same name for all the computers that you set up. You can see an example of this in Figure 3-15. Click **Next** when you are finished.

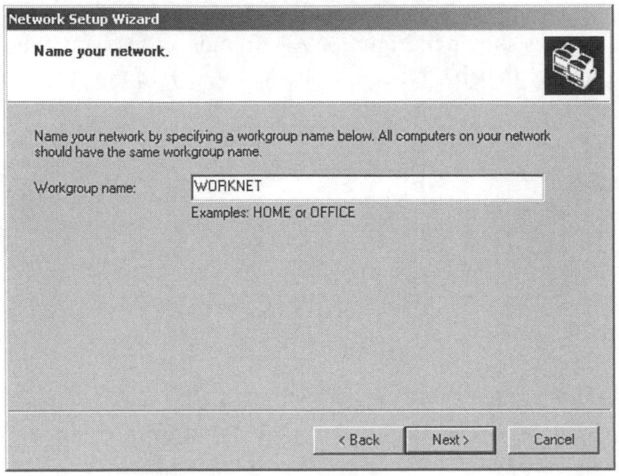

FIGURE 3-15   Network Name

STEP 6.   Now you will be prompted to turn on file and printer sharing. You should select this radio button, as shown in Figure 3-16. Click **Next**.

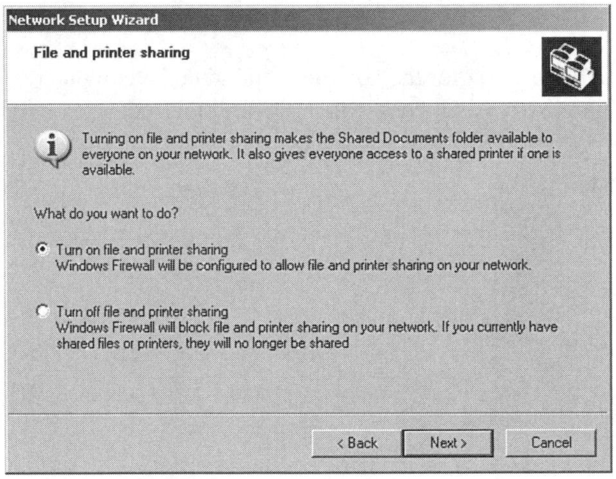

FIGURE 3-16   File and Printer Sharing

STEP 7.   You can now review your settings and use the Back button to make changes to any of these entries on the previous screens of the wizard. When you have reviewed the settings, click **Next**, and your PC will apply the network settings.

STEP 8.   After the settings have been applied, you will be asked whether you want to create a disk to apply these settings to other computers. For the purpose of this lab, you should select the **Just finish the wizard** option, as shown in Figure 3-17. Click **Next**.

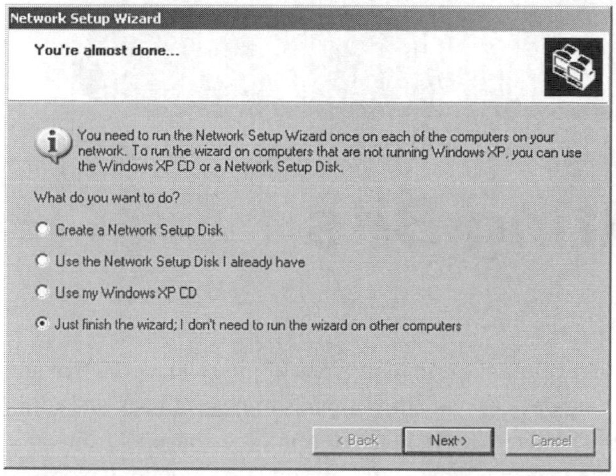

FIGURE 3-17   Final Selection

STEP 9.   When the final screen appears with further information, you can click **Finish** to end the wizard. You will then be prompted to restart your computer.

Lab 3.5 Review

1. What is the risk of enabling file sharing on your PC? Should this be enabled for every computer you use? Where can you access the folder you share? Use your textbook and Internet research to support your conclusion.

_____

_____

_____

_____

_____

_____

_____

2. Is there a risk to enabling a shared printer on your PC? Use your textbook and Internet research to justify your position.

_____

_____

_____

_____

_____

_____

_____

_____

_____

_____

_____

Chapter 4

Transmitting Bits

This chapter will allow you to explore the common types of physical media that are used to interconnect networking devices and allow signals to be sent back and forth between them. The labs in this chapter are designed to reinforce concepts from Chapter 4 of your *Introduction to Networking* textbook and allow you to explore some of the more important ideas with greater depth. You will explore the different types of network cabling that is commonly used and analyze the benefits and drawbacks of using each type. You will also explore some of the common problems in network media and create a hierarchy for investigating problems with media when they arise. At the end of this chapter, you should be able to

- Explain the various types of copper cabling used in networking and describe how to wire simple connections

- Explain the different modalities of fiber-optic cable and its application for long-distance communication

- Determine a hierarchy of cabling for a given network based on relative cost and distance

- Describe common wiring problems and create a troubleshooting plan for situations in which common problems occur

Lab 4.1: Copper Cabling

Approximate Lab Time: 20–25 min.

Materials Needed: Paper/Pencil, Textbook, and Internet Research

This lab reviews the basic standards and operation of copper cabling for network use. You will explore the standards for this type of cabling, review the common problems that you encounter with copper wire in live usage, and learn how to use placement to overcome some of them. Compile a lab report of the solutions to the assigned exercises and include a review of the work necessary to arrive at the solution.

Copper Cable Types and Standards

A network-capable computing device must contain a network interface card (NIC), a specialized piece of hardware that can translate information from the computer to transmit signals on the network media and recognize and translate incoming signals from the media to pass to the computer. Every NIC requires some form of physical access to the network media. A common example of this is an Ethernet port on a desktop or laptop computer. The physical port accepts a specific type of connector that aligns the network media with the NIC interface. The connectors exist at both ends of the media to allow devices to be connected to each other.

Exercise 4.1.1

Why are standards so important for NICs, connectors, and media? Use your textbook and Internet research to justify your answer.

_____

_____

_____

The oldest and cheapest form of cabling used as network media is copper wire. Aside from electrical wiring, it has been used for telephone cable, which itself is fundamental to the evolution of networking. Copper wire transmits electric signals efficiently, and it can handle enough voltage to power appliances or register just enough to transmit individual bits.

Exercise 4.1.2

The voltage for registering a bit of 1 on Ethernet can be as low as 2.5 volts or even 1 volt. Why is this so low when the capacity for transmitting electricity on the copper wire is so high? Use your textbook and Internet research to support your answer.

_____

_____

The first distinction of copper wire is shielded versus unshielded wire. The unshielded wire is cheaper, but it is more susceptible to interference than shielded wire. Unshielded wire is most common in network use because of its lower cost. To minimize the effects of interference, pairs of the copper wires in the cable are twisted around each other; this type of cabling is therefore called unshielded twisted-pair (UTP).

Exercise 4.1.3

What are some applications of shielded copper cable? Why is the more expensive shielded cable used in these situations? Use your textbook or Internet research to support your answer.

_____

_____

_____

Table 4-1 presents a partially complete list of attributes for the common UTP cabling standards. These different standards have evolved as network technology has improved and speed requirements have increased. These categories of UTP cable are what you will find in most Ethernet networks.

Table 4-1   UTP Standards

Category	Maximum Speed	Application
1	—	Telephone cabling (POTS)
2	4 Mbps	Token Ring
3		
4		
5		
5e	1 Gbps	Gigabit Ethernet
6		
6a		

Exercise 4.1.4

Complete the entries in Table 4-1. Use your textbook and Internet research to compose your answer.

The common connector for interfacing UTP wires to a computer for networking is the Registered Jack 45 (RJ-45) interface. This uses eight copper wires (four twisted pairs) to complete the connection between interfaces. The pinout for these wires defines the order in which the individual wires connect to the network interface card and how the wires transition from one end of the cable to the other. A straight cable is used to connect a device to a network hub or switch. This type of cable does not change the wiring order from one end to the other. You can see an example of this in Figure 4-1.

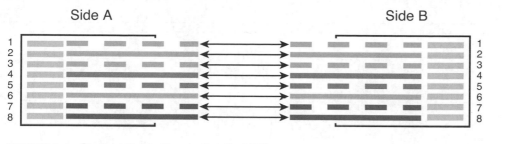

FIGURE 4-1   Straight Cable Connection for UTP

Another way to look at the pinout is through the color coding for the individual wires inside the cable and how they connect to the pin numbers of the connector. You can see the color coding for a straight cable pinout in Table 4-2.

Table 4-2   Straight Cable Color Coding for UTP

Pin	Side A	Side B
1	Orange-white	Orange-white
2	Orange	Orange
3	Green-white	Green-white
4	Blue	Blue
5	Blue-white	Blue-white
6	Green	Green
7	Brown-white	Brown-white
8	Brown	Brown

Exercise 4.1.5

A crossover cable is a type of cable used to connect similar devices, such as one computer connecting directly to another computer. Using Figure 4-1 and Table 4-2 as an example, create the diagram and color coding for a crossover cable. Use your textbook and Internet research to compose your answer. Hint: The crossover cable is more complex than simply reversing the entire set of wires. You are wiring the input pins to the output pins and vice versa.

The other type of copper cable with which you should be familiar is coaxial cable. Coaxial cable uses a single copper wire surrounded by shielding to transmit an analog signal. This type of cable is common in television wiring and is used in networking to deliver Internet connectivity over television cable from a service provider. Coaxial cable can also be used for Ethernet and has a longer maximum distance limit than UTP.

Exercise 4.1.6

Briefly describe the layered construction of a coaxial cable from the inner core to the outer insulation. Use your textbook and Internet research to compose your answer.

Cable Planning and Testing

The common UTP cables have an upper distance limit of 100 meters (or approximately 328 feet). This is because of attenuation. Attenuation is the loss of signal over distance. You can correct this attenuation with signal repeaters or equipment such as a hub, but they are expensive devices compared to the cost of the cable itself. You need to plan the types of cable you will need to connect devices (such as straight cables and crossover cables) and the category of UTP cable you should use for your network.

Exercise 4.1.7

Based solely on the distance limitation of UTP cable, what should you guarantee about any network you plan for UTP cable? Use your textbook and Internet research to justify your answer.

_____

_____

_____

Consider the network shown in Figure 4-2 for the following exercises. You can assume that the protocols in use and the type of routing equipment will not affect your answers. The distances are indicated on the lines. The lines are not drawn to scale with each other.

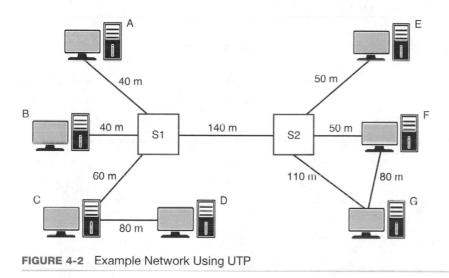

FIGURE 4-2 Example Network Using UTP

Exercise 4.1.8

What type of cable is necessary for each connection in Figure 4-2: straight or crossover? You can assume that S1 and S2 do not have the ability to resolve crossovers (called Auto-MDIX). Use your textbook and Internet research to compose your answer.

_____

_____

_____

_____

_____

Exercise 4.1.9

If all the connections in the network from Figure 4-2 use UTP cable, will they all be able to communicate correctly? If not, which links will not function and what should be done to resolve the issue? Use your textbook and Internet research to justify your answer.

_____

_____

_____

In addition to network planning, it is important to be able to test the basic connectivity of devices when you connect new media. Fortunately, UTP cable is widely adopted, and the devices used to test its connectivity are readily available and mostly inexpensive.

Exercise 4.1.10

Briefly describe the purpose of each of the following network testing devices:

- Multimeter
- Tone generator
- Pair scanner
- Time domain reflectometer (TDR)

For each device, use the Internet to find a vendor for the product and list its cost.

_____

_____

_____

_____

_____

_____

_____

Lab 4.1 Review

1. Modern routing devices have a software solution to detect crossover (called Auto-MDIX) and correct for it, allowing the use of straight cables to connect these devices instead of crossover cables. What is the benefit of this functionality for wiring a network?

_____

_____

_____

_____

_____

_____

_____

2. Signal repeaters will take the weak signal as input and retransmit it as a stronger signal. Why should these devices be placed before the end of the maximum distance for the cable?

_____

_____

_____

3. What is the limiting factor for the number of network connections a desktop or laptop computer can make?

_____

_____

_____

Lab 4.2: Fiber-Optic Cables

Approximate Lab Time: 10–15 min.
Prerequisite: Lab 4.1

Materials Needed: Paper/Pencil, PC Lab (Windows), Textbook, and Internet Research

This lab reviews the means by which signals are sent over fiber-optic cables. Fiber-optic cable can cross larger distances than copper wire with less risk of interference, but it is much more expensive to use. You will explore the different modalities for this type of cabling and review the deployment factors for both single-mode fiber (SMF) and multimode fiber (MMF). Compile a lab report of the solutions to the assigned exercises and include a review of the work necessary to arrive at the solution.

Singe-Mode Fiber

Fiber-optic cable is useful for covering large distances in a network. A single-mode fiber (SMF) uses a laser to transmit bits (detected by the presence or absence of light) over a thin filament of glass. The glass filament itself is somewhat flexible but brittle, so it needs to be insulated. A layer called cladding covers the fiber to strengthen it and eliminate external light from entering the glass core. This cladding layer is reflective and acts like a mirror to bounce light back into the core as the fiber bends. This is coated and surrounded by strengthening fibers to further protect the fragile fiberglass core. All of these layers are then wrapped in a plastic jacket.

Exercise 4.2.1

The light in an SMF cable travels down the center of the fiber parallel to the direction of the fiber in a single path. Can this type of cable be used to transmit and receive bits simultaneously, or does it require one fiber for transmitting and one for receiving? Justify your answer using your textbook and Internet research.

_____

_____

_____

_____

Exercise 4.2.2

What characteristics of fiber-optic cables allow them to be used over longer distances with less risk than copper cable?

_____

_____

_____

_____

Multimode Fiber

Multimode fiber (MMF) is a cheaper alternative to SMF. It has a larger glass core than SMF, so the light has multiple paths by which it can reach its destination. This means that the light source does not have to be as concentrated as SMF requires. You can see an illustration of this difference in Figure 4-3.

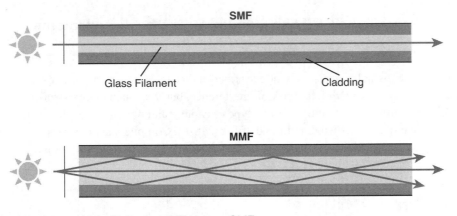

FIGURE 4-3   Light Paths in MMF Versus SMF

Exercise 4.2.3

MMF distances can still far exceed copper cable, but MMF cannot match the distance available from the more expensive SMF. What is the reason for the distance limitation with the use of MMF?

_____

_____

_____

_____

Lab 4.2 Review

1. What is the bend radius for a fiber-optic cable? Why is it important to adhere to the bend radius restrictions for fiber-optic cable?

   _____

   _____

   _____

   _____

2. Fiber-optic cables are often bundled together into thicker cables for wiring multiple devices in a location or to travel over long distances. What layers of the standard fiber-optic cable are necessary for each individual glass filament in order for them to be bundled together with other fibers?

   _____

   _____

   _____

   _____

Lab 4.3: Cabling Exploration

Approximate Lab Time: 15–20 min.
Prerequisite: Lab 4.2

Materials Needed: Paper/Pencil, Textbook, and Internet Research

This lab builds upon the previous labs and allows you to explore how different types of cabling can be used in a network to connect devices. Each type of cable has its strengths and weaknesses, and it is important to know when certain types should be applied. You will construct a general hierarchy of cables in this lab and use it to solve specific connection problems for example networks. Compile a lab report of the solutions to the assigned exercises and include a review of the work necessary to arrive at the solution.

Creating a Cabling Hierarchy

Most networks that span a significant distance make use of multiple types of networking cable to interlink the required devices (or nodes). Knowing when and how to apply the right kind of media for the requirements and price constraints of a network is essential to successful network planning. For this, you can create a general cabling hierarchy to use in finding solutions to match cabling to specific connection needs. You can see a partial table of the wiring that you have already studied in Table 4-3.

Table 4-3   Cabling Comparison Table

Type	Maximum Distance	Maximum Speed	Cost	Pros	Cons
UTP	100 m	1 Gbps	Low	Easy to install, inexpensive, NICs are common in devices	Limited distance, subject to interference
Coaxial (Thinnet)		100 Mbps			
Coaxial (Thicknet)		100 Mbps			
MMF	2 km+				
SMF	10 km+				

Exercise 4.3.1

Use your textbook and Internet research to complete the comparison in Table 4-3. Cite the sources from which you retrieved the information to complete the comparison.

Exercise 4.3.2

Rank the three main types of cable (UTP, SMF, and MMF) in a hierarchy of use for connecting network devices based on your completed comparison table. Use your textbook and Internet research to justify your ranking.

_____

_____

_____

_____

_____

Matching Cabling to Connection Needs

For the three networks presented in this section, you will create a network plan by choosing the type of cable to use for each connection. Use your comparison table and hierarchy to decide which cabling solution would work best in each case. You can assume a cost structure as outlined in Table 4-4.

Table 4-4   Cost Structure for Network Examples

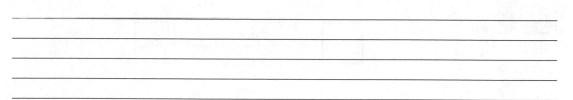

Device/Cable	Price
UTP	$0.25 per meter
Coaxial (Thinnet)	$0.27 per meter
Coaxial (Thicknet)	$0.27 per meter
MMF	$0.35 per meter
SMF	$0.45 per meter
Switch	$140
Coaxial NIC (PC)	$60
MMF NIC (PC)	$120
SMF NIC (PC)	$160
Coaxial NIC expansion card	$40
MMF NIC expansion card	$100
SMF NIC expansion card	$150

For these exercises, the PCs all have a preinstalled Ethernet port (for UDP cable). Switches can accommodate up to eight Ethernet (UTP) connections, and routers can handle six Ethernet (UTP) connections. Switches and routers have two expansion bays for additional NICs to be added.

Network A: The business owner of the network is interested in the overall cost of the network. He is willing to sacrifice speed for the sake of saving money. He has a large factory with offices at both ends. The cable between the offices will pass by a large volume of electric machinery, which will cause significant interference on any copper wiring solution. You can see the layout of Network A in Figure 4-4.

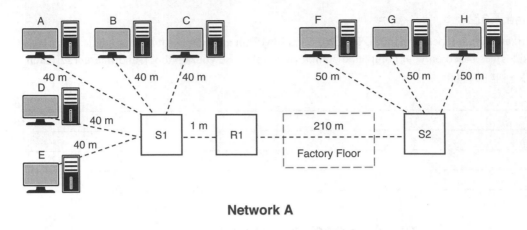

Network A

FIGURE 4-4   Network A

Exercise 4.3.3

Using the description of Network A and Figure 4-4, create a cabling solution for this network that meets the owner's needs. Justify your choices.

_____

_____

_____

_____

_____

_____

_____

_____

_____

_____

_____

_____

_____

Network B: The owner of this network is looking to connect three different design and construction sites together over a significant distance (permits have been obtained to install and bury the wire beyond the locations in the public space). The PCs and traffic for each site are minimal most of the time, but it is mission critical that they be able to communicate with each other quickly and exchange a large volume of information in short bursts. She is not as concerned with cost as she is with network speed and reliability. There are three routers (one for each site) that need to be connected, but they do not require a full mesh to function. You can see the layout of Network B in Figure 4-5.

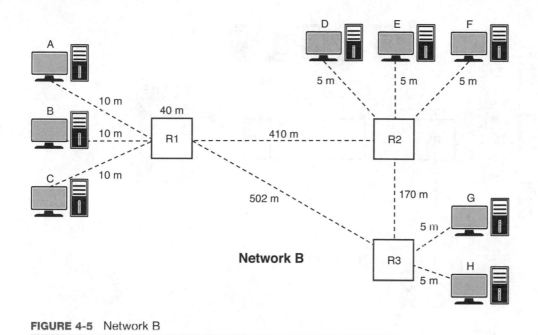

FIGURE 4-5 Network B

Exercise 4.3.4

Using the description of Network B and Figure 4-5, create a cabling solution for this network that
meets the owner's needs. Choose whether you want to connect the three routers in full mesh and
explain your choice. Justify your choices.

_____
_____
_____
_____
_____
_____
_____
_____
_____
_____
_____
_____

Network C: The owner of this network wants to create a network within his office building. The
cable was not installed when the building was constructed, so there might be some interference
from electric wires in the walls. The office is small but the PCs in use are spread among different
departments. Traffic is unlikely to be significant between the departments, and cost is a higher
concern than performance. You can see the layout of Network C in Figure 4-6.

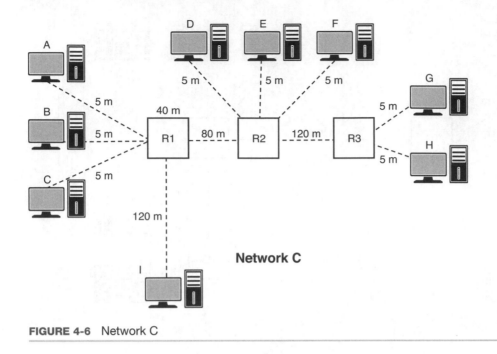

FIGURE 4-6   Network C

Exercise 4.3.5

Using the description of Network C and Figure 4-6, create a cabling solution for this network that meets the owner's needs. Justify your choices.

_____

_____

_____

_____

_____

_____

_____

Lab 4.3 Review

1. As the cost of copper increases and the cost of fiber-optic cable decreases, eventually fiber might be less expensive for local network connections than copper cable. What are some barriers to widespread adoption of fiber in place of UTP?

_____

_____

_____

_____

_____

_____

_____

2. Most wireless devices for home and small office use have an effective broadcast radius of 35 meters (or approximately 115 feet) and can share up to approximately 25 devices (though for voice and video, it is recommended to reduce this to 10–15 devices) per access point (AP). How would this fit into your cabling hierarchy as a networking solution?

_____

_____

_____

_____

_____

_____

_____

Lab 4.4: Cable Troubleshooting

Approximate Lab Time: 15–20 min.
Prerequisite: Lab 4.3

Materials Needed: Paper/Pencil, PC Lab (Windows), Textbook, and Internet Research

Whenever you install network media, it is important to know how to troubleshoot the connection if a problem occurs. There are various levels of troubleshooting, but it is always preferable to attempt a software solution before you have to start examining the cables themselves. This lab reviews basic troubleshooting operation for cable connections in a network and allows you to create a general troubleshooting plan for testing connections. Compile a lab report of the solutions to the assigned exercises and include a review of the work necessary to arrive at the solution.

Identify Device Problems

It is always preferable to be able to correct a networking issue through software instead of having to correct, replace, or rewire cable. You will learn about using the command line to troubleshoot networks and identify problems with connectivity in the next chapter, but for now, you will learn how to determine whether your own network interfaces on your PC are working correctly and how to restart them in case there is a problem. Not all issues can be corrected with software, but it makes a much more convenient place to start than to run down and evaluate cabling. To evaluate the status of your installed network interface cards and adapters, follow these steps:

STEP 1. Open the Control Panel from the **Start** menu. Choose **System** from the selection.

STEP 2. When the System Properties dialog box opens, choose the Hardware tab, as shown in Figure 4-7.

FIGURE 4-7   System Properties Dialog Box

STEP 3.   Click the **Device Manager** button. This opens a new Device Manager dialog box. You can see an example of this in Figure 4-8.

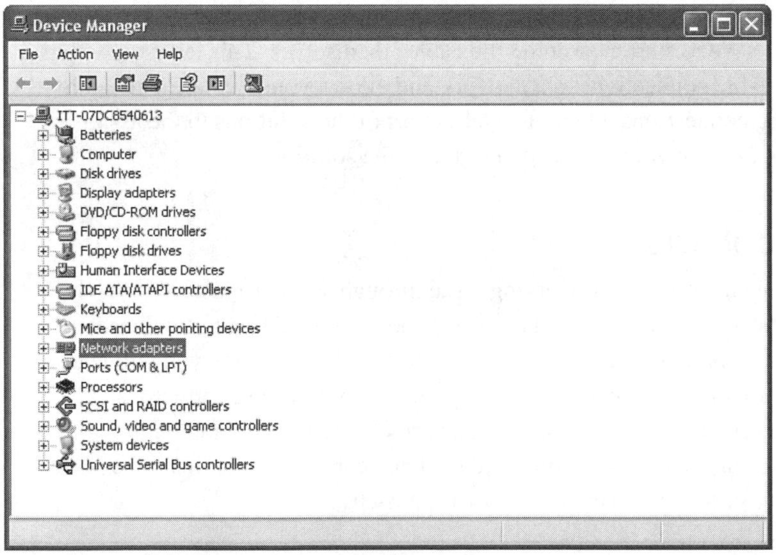

FIGURE 4-8   Device Manager Dialog Box

STEP 4.   Click the icon to expand the **Network adapters** entry in the Device Manager dialog box. This will display all the network adapters that you have available on your machine.

> **NOTE:** On a virtual machine, you will only see the adapter that you have for bridging the network to your live PC.

STEP 5.   Choose one of the available adapters and double-click the name. This opens the device details in a new window. You can see an example of this in Figure 4-9. You can restart a device by choosing **Disable** and then choosing **Enable** in the Device Usage selection box.

FIGURE 4-9   Device Detail for a Network Adapter

Exercise 4.4.1

What information about the device is displayed in the dialog box? What options are available under Device Usage?

_____

_____

_____

_____

Exercise 4.4.2

The tabs across the top of the dialog box provide additional information on the status of the device. Click the Advanced tab; what properties can be set from this tab? Click the Driver tab; this provides information on the software that controls the hardware adapter. What information is available for the device driver? How do you update the driver?

_____

_____

_____

_____

Identify Wiring Problems

When you cannot identify an issue from software, you will need to use hardware tools to test your network for functionality. Ideally you will be able to use the software tools to narrow the source of the problem to one of a small number of cables that could be causing the issue. There are certain problems in a network that cannot be identified by the host machine or even routing equipment. Physically checking these cables is the only way to determine the issue. The tools that you identified in Exercise 4.1.10 are a good place to start for checking connections in a network. The same tools you use to verify implementation can be used to check the status after the network is operational.

Exercise 4.4.3

The following list represents common problems in network media that cannot be easily determined by software applications and commands. For each entry, define the problem and list the types of cable (UTP, coaxial, SMF, and/or MMF) to which it applies. Use your textbook and Internet research to compose your answers.

- Noise
- Crosstalk
- Interference
- Open (open circuit)
- Short (short circuit)
- Break

Creating a Troubleshooting Plan

It is generally a good idea to create a troubleshooting plan for any issues that arise in a network. This will allow you to be systematic in your approach to solving the problem. You will grow this list as you get further in your textbook, but you can start with the simple tasks of checking a single PC for connectivity and then moving on to testing the individual media connections.

Exercise 4.4.4

In your own words, describe the troubleshooting plan for your own PC that you have established based on your explorations in this chapter.

_____

_____

Exercise 4.4.5

There are several general strategies that you can adopt when you do not have a clear idea of what the problem is with a network. Most of these use the OSI model to plan the information gathering and troubleshooting. Define and describe the following common troubleshooting strategies in relation to the OSI model:

- Bottom Up
- Top Down

_____

_____

_____

_____

_____

Lab 4.4 Review

1. Another troubleshooting strategy is known as Divide and Conquer. It requires that you have some knowledge of the problem before you begin. When would this strategy be most useful, and what is the benefit of being able to use it?

   _____

   _____

   _____

2. Why is it more efficient to check the status of network connections through software and command lines first before checking the physical hardware? When is it necessary to test the physical cable?

   _____

   _____

   _____

Chapter 5

Ethernet LANs

This chapter will allow you to explore the common LAN standards associated with wired Ethernet connections. You will also further explore command-line networking and troubleshooting. The labs in this chapter are designed to reinforce concepts from Chapter 5 of your *Introduction to Networking* textbook and allow you to explore some of the more important ideas with greater depth. You will review and assess the different Ethernet standards and IEEE LAN standards. You will also view live network packets and compare them to the command-line networking results to see how the command line is actualized in a network. You will also learn basic troubleshooting from the command-line interface. At the end of this chapter, you should be able to

- Identify and explain the common LAN terminology and standards
- Identify the MAC and IP addresses of your PC from the command line
- Determine your network settings from the command line
- Use command-line networking for basic troubleshooting on a network

Lab 5.1: LAN Standards

Approximate Lab Time: 15–20 min.

Materials Needed: Paper/Pencil, Textbook, and Internet Research

This lab reviews the basic IEEE Ethernet standards and the cabling and distance limitations defined by the more popular standards from the 802.3 family in use today. You will research these standards to learn more about the standards process and what is provided. Recall that standards are used to provide vendor independence in networking, which allows devices to connect based on a predetermined set of conditions regardless of its manufacturer; this is inherent and essential to modern networking. Compile a lab report of the solutions to the assigned exercises and include a review of the work necessary to arrive at the solution.

Ethernet Standards

The IEEE 802.3 group of standards is used to define wired Ethernet, the most common form of data link layer connectivity in modern networking. Ethernet uses frames and routes them locally through Media Access Control (MAC) addresses. Ethernet frames typically do not cross network boundaries. Instead, routing devices must remove the Ethernet frame from one network and apply a new frame for use in the next network in routing. Note that newer technologies like Metro Ethernet do allow frames to cross network boundaries.

Exercise 5.1.1

The IEEE standards cover more than just Ethernet. The 802.3 standard actually builds upon the 802.1 network architecture standard from IEEE. Briefly define the 802.1 standard and what it provides. Use your textbook and the Internet to research your answer.

_____

_____

_____

Exercise 5.1.2

The 802.3 family of standards has the format 802.3x where x is a sequence of letters specifying the new standards added to the 802.3 base standard. One of the enhancements to Ethernet is Power over Ethernet (PoE), in which Ethernet cable can provide power to remote, low-power devices that are not near an electrical outlet. What 802.3 standard originally defined PoE functionality? When was the standard enhanced, and what was the new standard name given for the enhancement? Use your textbook and the Internet to research your answer.

_____

_____

_____

Ethernet Technologies

There are a number of common standards defining the type of Ethernet in use and its associated physical media and distance limitation. The distance limitation is reflective of the type of media used. Whenever the Ethernet standard uses UTP, it requires certain categories of UTP wire to accommodate the expected speed of the network. You can see a partial list of the Ethernet technologies associated with these standards in Table 5-1.

Table 5-1   Ethernet Technology Listing

Standard	Cabling	Maximum Length
10BASE5	Coaxial (Thicknet)	
10BASE2	Coaxial (Thinnet)	
10BASE-T	UTP (Cat3, 5, 5e, 6)	
100BASE-FX		400 m
100BASE-T		
100BASE-T4		
100BASE-TX		
1000BASE-LX		
1000BASE-SX		220 m or 550 m (dependent upon fiber thickness)
1000BASE-ZX		100 km
1000BASE-T		

Exercise 5.1.3

Complete Table 5-1 by researching the various Ethernet standards and their associated properties. You can use your textbook and the Internet to determine the answers.

Exercise 5.1.4

What does the numeric prefix before BASE in the Ethernet standards define? Use your textbook and the Internet to research your answer. What does the inclusion of a postfix of -T imply?

_____

_____

_____

_____

_____

Lab 5.1 Review

1. If a 10BASE-T network (network A) was connected through a router to a 100BASE-T network (network B), what would the maximum speed of traffic be from a node in network A to a node in network B? Use your textbook and the Internet to research and justify your answer.

   _____

   _____

   _____

   _____

2. How is it possible for a network to uphold a maximum speed when it allows different categories of UTP wire to be used (such as Cat3, Cat5, and Cat5e)? Use your textbook and the Internet to research and justify your answer.

   _____

   _____

   _____

   _____

   _____

   _____

Lab 5.2: MAC and IP Addresses

Approximate Lab Time: 20–25 min.

Materials Needed: Paper/Pencil, PC Lab (Windows), Textbook, and Internet Research

This lab reviews network addressing at the data link layer and network layer for a device. You will explore MAC address structure and learn how to determine the manufacturer of a NIC from the MAC address. This lab also covers the basic structure of an IP address and describes how you can identify it in network information at the command line. Both of these address values are necessary to interpret the results of the Address Resolution Protocol (ARP), which is used to resolved a MAC address from an IP address. Compile a lab report of the solutions to the assigned exercises and include a review of the work necessary to arrive at the solution.

MAC Address Structure

The Media Access Control (MAC) address is a unique physical address for each NIC. This address is encoded in the read-only memory (ROM) of the NIC and, ideally, is not subject to change (though some vendors do allow this). The MAC address is 48 bits in length (6 bytes) and is commonly represented as 12 hexadecimal characters (separated by hyphens or colons depending upon the application). You can see an example of a MAC address in Figure 5-1. The first 24 bits are the manufacturer's Organizationally Unique Identifier (OUI); the last 24 bits are uniquely assigned by the manufacturer for each NIC that it produces.

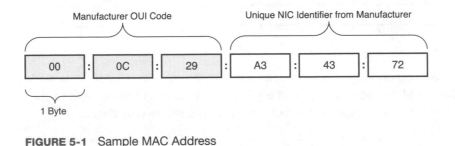

FIGURE 5-1   Sample MAC Address

Exercise 5.2.1

Why must a MAC address be unique for every NIC produced? What effect will it have on the network if two devices from two different manufacturers share the last 24 bits of their MAC addresses? Explain your answer. Use your textbook and the Internet to research your answer.

_____

_____

_____

_____

_____

_____

_____

_____

_____

_____

_____

_____

_____

_____

Every NIC has its own MAC address, so you will have a unique MAC address for each network adapter present on your computer. To determine the MAC address of a network interface on your Windows PC, follow these steps:

STEP 1.   Open the Control Panel and choose Network Connections. Double-click one of the connections. A new window will appear with the status of the network connection. You can see an example of this in Figure 5-2.

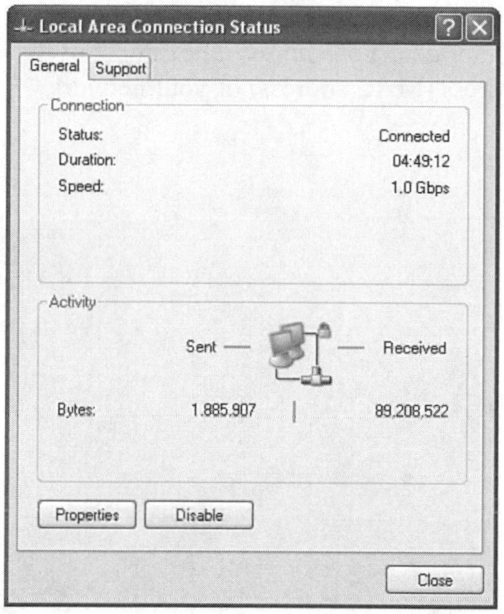

FIGURE 5-2   Sample Network Adapter Status Window

STEP 2.   Click the **Support** tab at the top of the window. You can see an example of this in Figure 5-3.

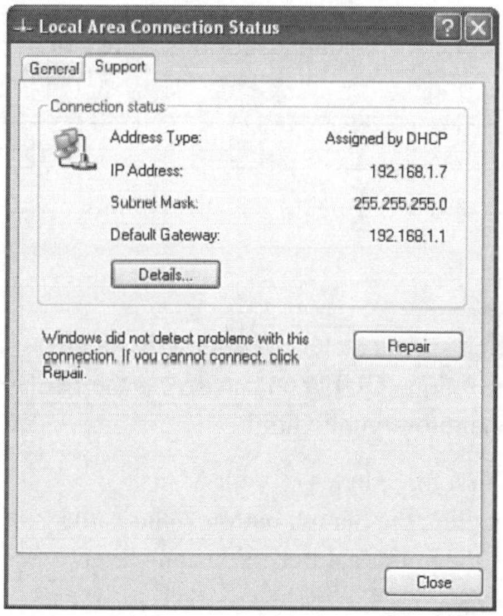

FIGURE 5-3   Support Tab of the Network Status Window

Exercise 5.2.2

What information about the network connection is given on the Support tab of the status window?

_____

_____

STEP 3. Click the **Details** button on the **Support** tab. This will open a new window with the complete connection information for the network interface. You can see an example of this in Figure 5-4. This window shows the physical address (MAC address) of your network adapter.

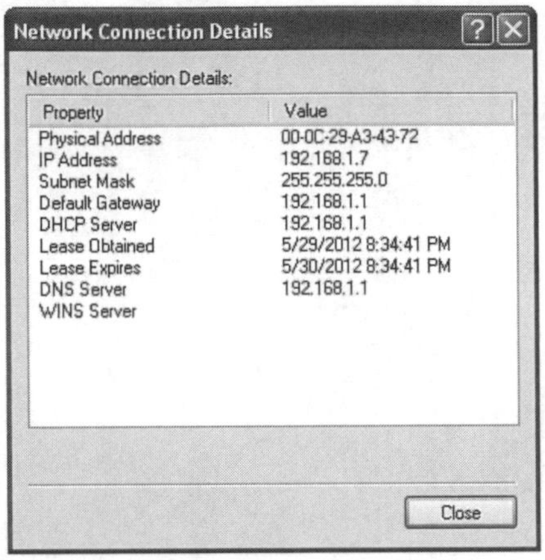

FIGURE 5-4 Connection Details Window

Exercise 5.2.3

What is the physical address (the MAC address) of the NIC (or network adapter) for this connection?

____

____

____

Exercise 5.2.4

You can determine the manufacturer of your NIC using the first six characters of your MAC address. To do this, you must search the IEEE records database for the unique OUI. You can access the IEEE database at this address: http://standards.ieee.org/develop/regauth/oui/public.html.

On this page, you should locate the search box and enter the first three bytes of your MAC address separated by hyphens (such as "00-0C-44"), and then click the Search button. Who is the manufacturer for your NIC? What information is given about the manufacturer? You can see an example record returned from this site in Figure 5-5.

____

____

```
00-0C-29   (hex)              VMware, Inc.
000C29     (base 16)          VMware, Inc.
                              3401 Hillview Avenue
                              Palo Alto CA 94304
                              UNITED STATES
```

FIGURE 5-5 Sample IEEE NIC Manufacturer Record

Basic IP Addressing

Internet Protocol (IP) addressing is a subject for later chapters, but it is necessary to understand the structure and appearance of an IP address to make use of some of the networking commands that allow you to explore your local network and reach remote resources. An IP address is a logical address that is uniquely assigned to a single device on any interconnected network. The most common version of an IP address is an IPv4 address, which consists of 4 bytes arranged into quadrants. Unlike MAC addresses, IP addresses are represented in decimal, so each quadrant can consist of the numbers 0 through 255. You can see an example of an IP address in Figure 5-6.

> **NOTE:** Not all possible IP addresses are valid, and not all of them can be routed. For now, you should focus on the structure of the IP address and understand how to recognize these addresses when you encounter them.

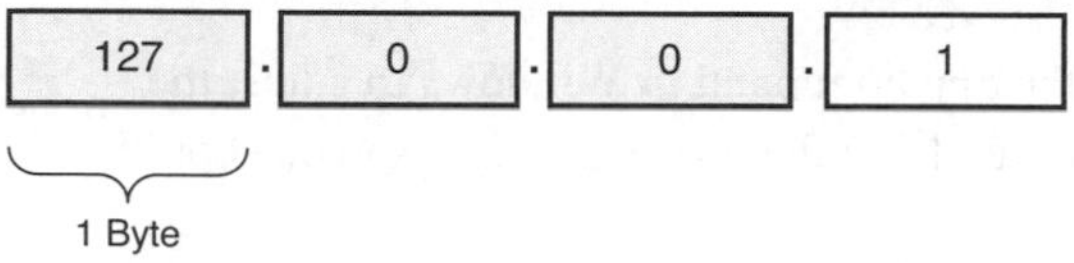

| 127 | . | 0 | . | 0 | . | 1 |

1 Byte

FIGURE 5-6   IP Address Structure

Exercise 5.2.5

You can view your IP address for a NIC (or network adapter) by double-clicking one of the available connections in the Network Connections window (accessible from the Control Panel) and selecting the Support tab, just as you did when you were finding your MAC address. This information is also given in the Details window where you found the MAC address. What is the IP address of your NIC or network adapter? What is the IP address listed for your default gateway?

> **NOTE:** When your IP address is 127.0.0.1, it means that you are not connected to any network; this is the local host address.

Using ARP

The Address Resolution Protocol (ARP) is used to resolve a logical (IP) address to a physical (MAC) address. This protocol is used often when new routes are needed or a new IP address is encountered by your network device where traffic needs to be routed. You can use the **arp** command on a Windows machine to view the current MAC address table and to add and remove IP/MAC pairs in the list.

Exercise 5.2.6

Use your textbook and the Internet to determine the communication steps in an ARP Request and Response. What steps are involved and how is each message sent (broadcast to all devices or unicast to a single device)?

_____

_____

_____

_____

_____

_____

_____

_____

_____

_____

For the rest of this lab, you will be practicing using the **arp** command in Windows to adjust the address table of your machine. The **arp** command is used from the command line, so you should open a new command-line window on your PC.

Exercise 5.2.7

The argument **-a** will display the IP/MAC paired address table for the computer. In the command window, type the following command and record the results:

```
arp -a
```

_____

_____

Exercise 5.2.8

Most ARP requests are dynamic when a new destination is encountered. You can also add static entries to your address table using the **-s** argument for the **arp** command. This takes the form of a MAC and IP address pairing. Enter the following at the command line to add a new static entry to your address table:

```
arp -s 10.0.0.8 00-AA-00-AA-BB-CC
```

Run the command **arp -a** again to see the effect it has on the table. What is the IP address that is added? What is the MAC address that was added? Use the **-s** argument to add a new address to the table to match the IP address 101.0.0.1 to the MAC address 00-AA-00-11-11-11. What command did you use to add the address pair? What is displayed as the type for these pairs?

_____

_____

_____

_____

_____

_____

Exercise 5.2.9

In addition to setting an address pair manually, you can also use the **-d** argument for the **arp** command to remove address pairs from the table by specifying an IP address. After completing Exercise 5.2.8, you should have two static addresses in the ARP address table. Use the following command to remove the entry you placed in Exercise 5.2.8:

```
arp -d 10.0.0.8
```

Use the **arp -a** command to verify that the entry is removed. What command will you use to remove the pairing to MAC address 00-AA-00-11-11-11 that you entered as a static pair in the table?

Lab 5.2 Review

1. The dynamic entries in an ARP cache are emptied after a few minutes of inactivity with a host. What is the reason for this and why is it beneficial? Use your textbook and the Internet to research your answer.

2. ARP requests are automatically sent as needed whenever a device connection is initiated without manually using the **arp** command. This occurs for any type of network connection. Why is this necessary for communication across devices? Use your textbook and Internet research to justify your answer.

3. What will happen if you attempt to remove an IP/MAC address pair from the ARP address table that is not there? You can specify an IP address after the **-a** argument to get the MAC address for the specific logical address. What happens when you request an address that is not in the cache?

Lab 5.3: Finding Network Settings

Approximate Lab Time: 15–20 min.
Prerequisite: Lab 5.2
Materials Needed: Paper/Pencil, PC Lab (Windows), Textbook, and Internet Research

This lab will explore the network settings for your connection to the local network using the command-line interface on a Windows machine; this is the professional method for troubleshooting networks and determining network information. You will use the command-line interface to gather information about your network devices and adapters as well as your default gateway and other networked resources. Learning these commands will help you as you progress to setting up a wireless local-area network (WLAN) in the next chapter. Compile a lab report of the solutions to the assigned exercises and include a review of the work necessary to arrive at the solution.

Using ipconfig

The **ipconfig** command will provide you with all the information you can get from using the Network Connections folder to check the status of your network connections and adapters on a Windows machine directly from the command-line interface. You can enter the code by itself to display connection information such as the IP address, default gateway (also an IP address), and subnet mask in use.

> **NOTE:** You should be familiar with this command and what it returns from the earlier lab in which you tested your ability to access the command line. This time, you should have a better understanding of the information it returns.
>
> Your default gateway is the device through which you connect to the Internet or any other interconnected networks.

You can add arguments to **ipconfig** to make it more useful for gathering and setting network information. There are two arguments in particular that you will practice here: **release** and **renew**.

Exercise 5.3.1

For this exercise, you will release your IP address using **ipconfig**. This is a beneficial tool for troubleshooting your own local network and correcting any problems with the assignment of IP addresses. This exercise requires that you have DHCP in use for assigning IP addresses, which is a typical default setting. To begin, you should type the command **ipconfig** at the command-line interface and press **Enter**. Record the information it presents for the IP address and default gateway; you can ignore the rest of the information for now.

When you have completed this, type the following command to release the IP address:

```
ipconfig /release
```

What information is displayed as a result?

_____

_____

To renew your lease on the IP address for your network card or adapter, you will use the following command:

```
ipconfig /renew
```

This will create a new lease on an IP address for your network card or adapter. When the command to renew the IP address is complete, you should compare the result to the initial run of **ipconfig** and compare the results. Are the entries the same for the IP address and for the default gateway?

_____

Using ping

The **ping** command is used to test connectivity between two hosts on a network (or interconnected network). On Windows machines, this is activated by entering **ping** at the command-line interface. However, **ping** requires arguments to function. In the exercises for this lab, you will explore the functionality and format of using the **ping** command.

Exercise 5.3.2

You can use the **ping** command on your local machine. This does not send traffic out onto the network, but it is an effective means of making sure that your network adapter is functional. To ping the local host, use the following command:

```
ping localhost
```

What address is returned as the IP address of localhost? How many times is the ping message sent by default?

_____

_____

_____

Exercise 5.3.3

For this exercise, you will ping the default gateway and two web addresses to see the difference in timing of the response. First, ping the default gateway (which you can get from running the **ipconfig** command if you forgot what it is) using the following format (replace the IP address given with the address of your default gateway):

```
ping 192.168.1.1
```

How much time (in the _time=_ part of the output) did it take for the ping response to come back to the local machine? If there were different values, report the average response time.

_____

_____

Next you will ping a destination farther away than your local network. You must have Internet connectivity enabled for this to work.

> **NOTE:** The **ping** command is a professional tool for troubleshooting and investigating networks, but most networks disable this message from crossing network boundaries because it has a high potential to clog the network.

Execute the following command from the command-line interface:

```
ping www.google.com
```

How much time (on average) did it take to get a response from the host? How does this compare to the time it took to get a response from the default gateway? Choose another web address and send a **ping** command to it. Did the **ping** command get a response? If so, how long did it take (on average)? What makes the difference in the timing of these messages?

_____

_____

_____

Exercise 5.3.4

For this exercise, you will use the **-a** argument for **ping**. This will force the **ping** command to return the host name as well as the IP address. To force a host name return, enter the following command (replacing the IP address with that of your default gateway):

```
ping -a 192.168.1.1
```

What is the name of the host for the default gateway? Use this argument to ping localhost. What name does it return?

_____

_____

_____

Exercise 5.3.5

You can use the **-n** argument and a number to specify the number of ping messages that should be sent. To ping the default gateway six times, enter the following command (again you should replace the IP address given with the IP address of your default gateway):

```
ping -n 6 192.168.1.1
```

What is the benefit of being able to send a set number of ping messages to a host? You can use your textbook and Internet research to compose your answer.

_____

_____

_____

Using tracert

The **tracert** command is used to determine the complete path between your machine and a network destination (to trace the route). In Windows, this command is given as **tracert**; this command requires a destination IP address or web address to work. The **tracert** command is an extension of the **ping** command, which pings each device in the path between the originating host and the destination host requesting a reply message.

Exercise 5.3.6

For this exercise, you will compare the **tracert** results for two different web addresses. To begin, though, you will start with running **tracert** to your default gateway with the following command (replacing the IP address shown with your default gateway IP address):

```
tracert 192.168.1.1
```

How many devices are returned in the path between your machine and the default gateway?

_____

_____

Now you will use the **tracert** command to access two different web hosts and compare the devices returned in the path. To begin, use the following command:

```
tracert www.google.com
```

Record the path that is returned from the host. Next, choose another web host (such as www.microsoft.com) and run the **tracert** command to it. Record the path that is returned. How many lines of the device path do these two hosts have in common? What do these devices represent?

_____

_____

_____

Using netstat

The **netstat** command is used to determine the network status of any currently active connections. This will return only recent activity because the cache for this empties as the active connections are closed. This is a helpful command to determine what protocols are in use and what hosts are being contacted by your machine.

Exercise 5.3.7

Run the **netstat** command (without any arguments) on your machine from the command-line interface. How many active connections are returned? What protocols are in use?

_____

_____

_____

Open a web browser such as Internet Explorer and enter a destination web address in the address bar. When this page has loaded, run the **netstat** command from the command-line interface again. How many connections are returned this time? Where did these connections originate? Use your textbook and Internet research to compose your answer.

_____

_____

_____

Lab 5.3 Review

1. The **ping** command has an argument, **-t**, that allows the ping to send messages repeatedly until it is manually stopped by a user pressing **Ctrl+C**. Why would this functionality be beneficial in networking? How could it be misused?

   _____

   _____

   _____

   _____

2. Running commands such as **ping** and **tracert** initiates connections to external hosts; this will also send ARP requests as the hosts are connected. Run one of these commands for a web host and then run the **arp -a** command. What IP/MAC address pairs are returned? Why is this the case?

   _____

   _____

   _____

Lab 5.4: Basic Network Troubleshooting

Approximate Lab Time: 15–20 min.
Prerequisite: Lab 5.3

Materials Needed: Paper/Pencil, PC Lab (Windows), Textbook, and Internet Research

This lab examines the use of basic commands used at the command line to troubleshoot a network. These commands are not inclusive enough to diagnose and solve all problems that you will encounter, but they can provide basic information to help you determine connectivity issues and gather information about the connected hosts. Compile a lab report of the solutions to the assigned exercises and include a review of the work necessary to arrive at the solution.

Network Troubleshooting from the Command Line

The command-line interface is a very powerful tool for diagnosing network problems. Using the commands that you have learned in Labs 5.2 and 5.3, you will examine a sample network and determine the commands that would give you the information you need to diagnose the problem on the network.

The sample network you will be using for this lab is shown in Figure 5-7. There are five PCs connected in a small office with a central router that connects the local network to the Internet through an Internet service provider (ISP). The router has two network interfaces, one for the local network and one for connecting to the ISP.

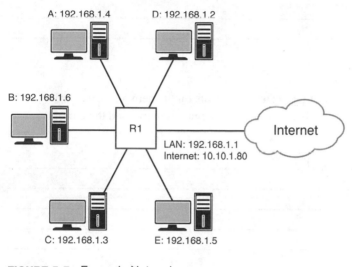

FIGURE 5-7   Example Network

Exercise 5.4.1

If you needed to determine the computer name used for node E on the network (starting from node A), what command would you use to get this information? Give the command sequence you would enter at the command line to retrieve this information.

Exercise 5.4.2

What is the best (easiest and most efficient) command to determine whether all the hosts on the local-area network are reachable? You can assume that you are starting from computer A. List the command sequence(s) you would need to enter to test this functionality.

Exercise 5.4.3

If your computer (node A) is unable to reach the Internet, what is the best way to determine where the error is occurring using command-line networking? Give the command sequence you would use to determine this.

_____

_____

Exercise 5.4.4

If your local machine (node A) is not connecting to any other hosts on the network, what two commands will give you information on whether your network device is active and the current configuration of your NIC or adapter?

_____

_____

_____

_____

_____

_____

_____

_____

Lab 5.4 Review

1. Using the sample network shown in Figure 5-7, what information should the ARP address cache contain for Router R1 assuming that all the machines are actively transmitting around the time of the command entry? Use your textbook and Internet research to support your answer.

_____

_____

_____

_____

_____

_____

2. If the problem with connectivity is located somewhere on the ISP, what steps should you take on your own network to correct the problem? Use your textbook and Internet research to support your answer.

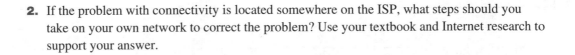

_____

_____

_____

_____

_____

Chapter 6

Wireless LANs

This chapter will allow you to explore the concepts of modern wireless networking. Though there are other wireless technologies such as infrared communication, this chapter focuses on wireless standards and technologies for radio frequency–based communication. The IEEE 802.11 set of standards defines this type of communication and interactivity among these devices. In this chapter, you will use the wireless Cisco routers and wireless USB adapters to join and configure wireless networks. You will learn about the placement and overlap of wireless channels as well. At the end of this chapter, you should be able to

- Identify and explain wireless domain types and the IEEE 802.11 standards
- Determine wireless networks within a broadcast radius and use the command line to gather network information
- Configure a wireless router for operation
- Plan a wireless infrastructure using appropriate antennas and channel selection

Lab 6.1: Wireless Broadcast Domains

Approximate Lab Time: 15–20 min.

Materials Needed: Paper/Pencil, Textbook, and Internet Research

This lab reviews the basic IEEE 802.11 family of standards for radio frequency wireless communication. You will compare the use of wireless technology with the use of cabled network technology. As part of this lab, you will examine the concept of a service set and shared wireless connections. Compile a lab report of the solutions to the assigned exercises and include a review of the work necessary to arrive at the solution.

Domain Types

Wireless technology has advanced greatly in recent years for use in networking. Today, most handheld smart phones and tablets are compatible with wireless networking technology through the IEEE 802.11 standards. The interoperability of wireless networks has been governed by an organization known as the Wi-Fi Alliance, which has sought to preserve vendor independence across wireless device manufacturers. Wireless networking involves the use of devices called access points (AP), which act to bridge the communication types from wireless devices to the wired portion of a network.

Exercise 6.1.1

A service set is the basic unit of a wireless network. It consists of an AP and one or more stations (commonly abbreviated STAs) that share the wireless communication channel. The STAs connect to the AP using a Service Set Identifier (SSID), which is transmitted by the AP to allow the STAs to connect.

There are two main types of service sets: Basic Service Sets (BSS) and Extended Service Sets (ESS). Define these two terms and identify where they are most useful. Use your textbook and Internet research to compose your answer.

_____

_____

_____

Wireless Standards

Similar to the IEEE 802.3 standards for wired Ethernet, the IEEE 802.11 standards define the common operation of radio frequency wireless networks. There are a number of standards in this family, but three are more commonly used than the rest for home and office use; these are the b, g, and n standards. Table 6-1 presents a partial list of the capabilities of each standard. The indoor maximum transmission distance is much shorter than the outdoor maximum transmission distance because of the walls and furniture through which the wireless signals must pass indoors.

Table 6-1   IEEE 802.11 Standards

Standard	Frequency (GHz)	Maximum Transmission Rate (Mbps)	Standard Indoor Transmission Range (m)	Standard Outdoor Transmission Range (m)
802.11a	5			
802.11b	2.4	11		
802.11g			38	140
802.11n				

Exercise 6.1.2

Using your textbook and the Internet, complete Table 6-1. In the case of frequencies, list all possible values.

Lab 6.1 Review

1. Another type of service set is the Independent Basic Service Set (IBSS), which does not require a central AP. How does this type of network function, and how is the SSID broadcast in this type of service set?

   _____

   _____

   _____

   _____

2. Another type of wireless connection is infrared (used for point-to-point communication called *beaming*). What is the limitation of this type of wireless communication? Why is radio frequency wireless communication superior in versatility and performance?

   _____

   _____

   _____

   _____

3. WLANs have a lower maximum speed than wired LANs, but most homes use WLAN technology instead of cabling to connect to an Internet service provider (ISP). What is the trade-off between WLAN and LAN technology? Why is WLAN technology appealing for home use?

   _____

   _____

   _____

   _____

   _____

Lab 6.2: Identifying WLANs

Approximate Lab Time: 15–20 min.
Prerequisite: Lab 6.1

Materials Needed: Paper/Pencil, PC Lab (Windows, USB Wireless Adapter, Cisco Linksys Router), Textbook, and Internet Research

This lab reviews wireless connectivity from the perspective of the PC (whether it is a laptop or desktop). Most new computers come equipped with embedded wireless network cards. The Windows operating system has the capability to manage this type of connection along with the wired Ethernet LAN connections you have already seen. This lab will review the detection and connection to a wireless network and describe how to determine the network settings when a wireless AP is detected. Compile a lab report of the solutions to the assigned exercises and include a review of the work necessary to arrive at the solution.

Detecting Wireless Broadcast Domains

Windows has a native manager for wireless networks. You can enable this when you connect an external wireless network adapter (such as a USB-connected device). Most external wireless network adapters also have their own associated utility and management tools. In this lab, you will look at both methods for managing wireless devices and determine the information provided by each.

Exercise 6.2.1

For this lab, you will need the external USB wireless adapter for your PC. Using the virtual machine, connect the device to the PC, right-click its icon in the VMware icon tray, and then choose Connect (Disconnect from Host). A sample of this tray and its available icons is shown in Figure 6-1.

> **NOTE:** You can also perform this lab and exploration with your own laptop or PC with either an external or a built-in wireless adapter. It is an interesting exercise to see the number of wireless networks broadcasting within your home or at a local coffee shop.

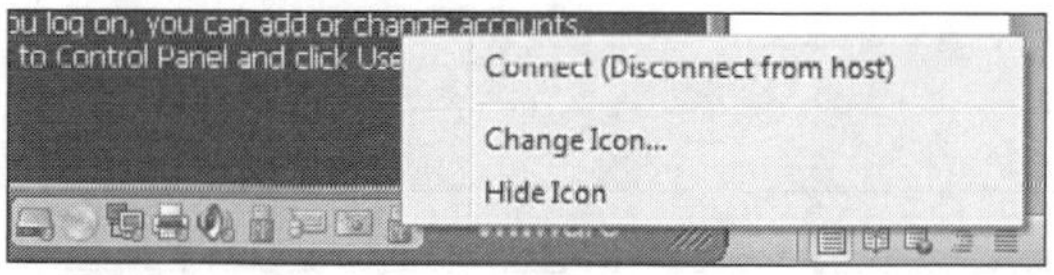

FIGURE 6-1 VMware Icon Tray

Your USB network adapter might be installed already. If it is not installed, you can follow the installation steps using the default settings for your device. You can alternately use the device on the host PC and bridge the network to your virtual machine (VM) using the LAN or Network Adapter icon in the VMware icon tray.

> **NOTE:** You might need to disable the bridged connection to the LAN from the host machine for the USB wireless adapter to function correctly. This is particularly true if the AP you are using does not connect to the Internet.

You can see an example of a software utility for managing wireless network connections in Figure 6-2. You can use the utility to connect to the available wireless networks, or you can allow Windows to manage the connection.

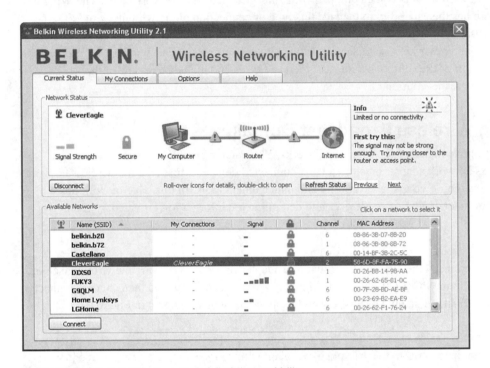

FIGURE 6-2   Belkin Wireless Network Adapter Utility

What information about the available wireless networks is given in the utility for the USB network adapter? If your USB device does not come with a utility, you can answer the question using the example in Figure 6-2.

_____

_____

_____

Your USB wireless adapter should also have the option to allow Windows to manage the connection to wireless networks. You should examine the utility options to determine how to change this setting. You can see an example of this in Figure 6-3.

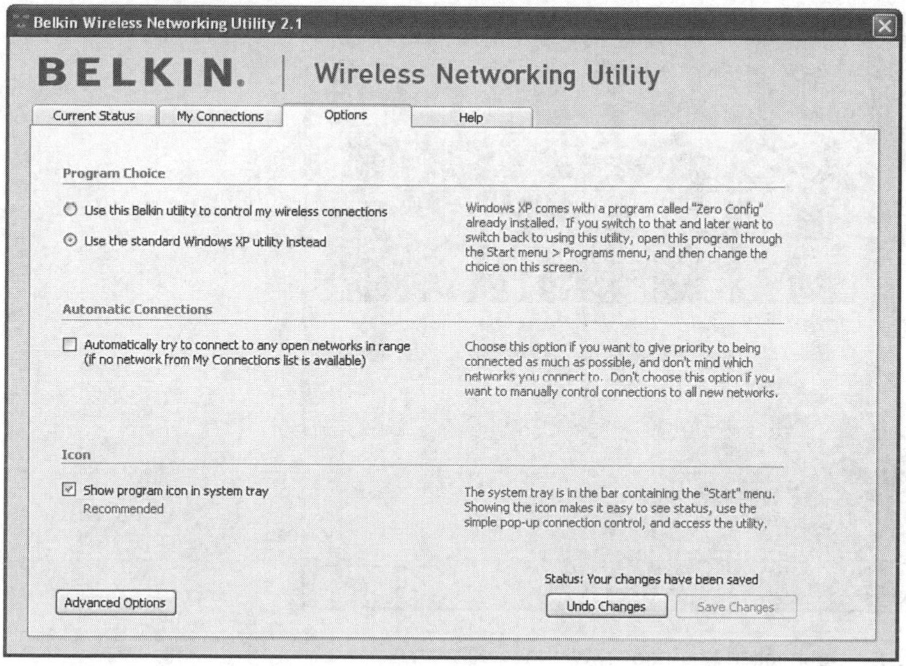

FIGURE 6-3 Changing Wireless Management to Windows

When you enable Windows to manage the wireless connections, you get a different network view. To see the available wireless networks in Windows, double-click the icon in the lower-right corner of the taskbar at the bottom of the screen that looks like a signal-strength gauge. This will open the wireless network selection window similar to what is shown in Figure 6-4. You can also open this from the Network Connections utility in the Control Panel.

> **NOTE:** The wireless network management tools are only available in a VMware PC if you have the USB wireless adapter connected to the VM; otherwise, the wireless network connections will be managed on the host machine.

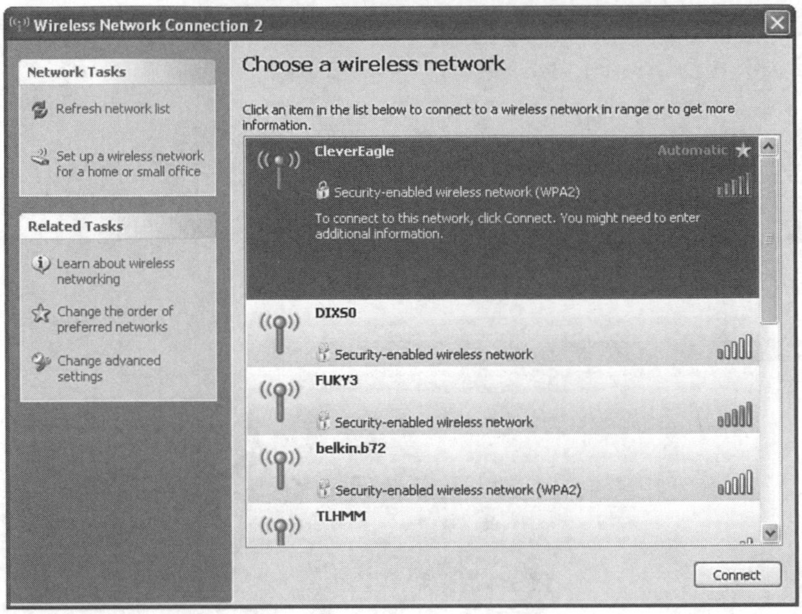

FIGURE 6-4 Wireless Connection Manager in Windows XP

What information is available about the wireless networks within broadcast range on the Windows wireless connection manager? How is this different from the information provided by the utility? When you select one of the available wireless networks that has security enabled, what information must you provide to connect to it?

_____

_____

_____

Using netsh for Wireless Networks

The network shell command-line utility in Windows is called netsh. You can use this utility to detect and modify network settings on your Windows machine. This command has uses for all types of networks, but it can be used to gather more detailed information on wireless networks than most utilities (including the Windows wireless connection manager) provide.

Exercise 6.2.2

The **netsh** command by itself will open the interactive mode for the command to allow you to enter individual commands for **netsh**. You can use the following command to determine the available contexts (used similar to command arguments) in **netsh**:

```
netsh ?
```

> **NOTE:** If you enter the **netsh** command by itself, you can exit the input stream to **netsh** by typing **quit** and pressing Enter.

The context that is necessary for managing wireless networks is called *wlan*. If you have this enabled, it will appear in the list provided. Not all the contexts for netsh are available on every machine. Sample output will be provided for these commands in case the wlan context is not available on your PC.

To enter a context, type the name of the context after the **netsh** command. Without additional arguments, the context name will list the available arguments for the context. You can see an example of this for wlan in the output that follows:

```
The following commands are available:
Commands in this context:
?               - Displays a list of commands.
add             - Adds a configuration entry to a table.
connect         - Connects to a wireless network.
delete          - Deletes a configuration entry from a table.
disconnect      - Disconnects from a wireless network.
dump            - Displays a configuration script.
export          - Saves WLAN profiles to XML files.
help            - Displays a list of commands.
refresh         - Refresh hosted network settings.
reportissues    - Generate WLAN smart trace report.
set             - Sets configuration information.
show            - Displays information.
start           - Start hosted network.
stop            - Stop hosted network.

To view help for a command, type the command, followed by a space, and then type ?.
```

The command you will use for gathering wireless information is shown. This will display the available information for wireless networks in range, just as the graphic utility did in the Windows wireless network connection manager. However, the **netsh** command can provide more detailed information. For basic information on the available wireless networks, you can use the following command:

```
netsh wlan show networks
```

An example of the output of this command is as follows:

```
Interface name : Wireless Network Connection
There are 9 networks currently visible.

SSID 1 : 1TGR4
    Network type            : Infrastructure
    Authentication          : Open
    Encryption              : WEP

SSID 2 : DIXS0
    Network type            : Infrastructure
    Authentication          : Open
    Encryption              : WEP

SSID 3 : Home Lynksys
    Network type            : Infrastructure
    Authentication          : WPA-Personal
    Encryption              : TKIP

SSID 4 : MA6U4
    Network type            : Infrastructure
    Authentication          : Open
    Encryption              : WEP
```

```
SSID 5 : TLHMM
    Network type             : Infrastructure
    Authentication           : WPA2-Personal
    Encryption               : CCMP

SSID 6 : PPP7C
    Network type             : Infrastructure
    Authentication           : Open
    Encryption               : WEP

SSID 7 : CleverEagle
    Network type             : Infrastructure
    Authentication           : WPA2-Personal
    Encryption               : CCMP

SSID 8 : Castellano
    Network type             : Infrastructure
    Authentication           : WPA-Personal
    Encryption               : TKIP

SSID 9 : FUKY3
    Network type             : Infrastructure
    Authentication           : Open
    Encryption               : WEP
```

What information is given by this command? How does this compare to the Windows wireless network manager? You can use the preceding sample output if the wlan context is not installed for netsh on your machine.

The real benefit of this command-line utility is with the use of the **all** argument for the **show** command. This will provide more detailed information on the wireless networks available. It will even show the wireless networks that are not broadcasting an SSID. The command for this is

```
netsh wlan show all
```

This command will display all the stored profiles for known network connections and the available networks. You can see an example of the output of this command showing only the available networks here:

```
=====================================================================
====================== SHOW NETWORKS MODE=BSSID ======================
=====================================================================
Interface name : Wireless Network Connection
There are 7 networks currently visible.

SSID 1 : Home Lynksys
    Network type             : Infrastructure
    Authentication           : WPA-Personal
    Encryption               : TKIP
    BSSID 1                  : 00:23:69:b2:ea:e9
        Signal               : 68%
        Radio type           : 802.11g
        Channel              : 6
        Basic rates (Mbps) : 1 2 5.5 11
        Other rates (Mbps) : 6 9 12 18 24 36 48 54
```

```
SSID 2 : MA6U4
    Network type              : Infrastructure
    Authentication           : Open
    Encryption               : WEP
    BSSID 1                  : 00:1f:90:c5:37:2c
        Signal               : 66%
        Radio type           : 802.11g
        Channel              : 11
        Basic rates  (Mbps)  : 1 2 5.5 11
        Other rates  (Mbps)  : 6 9 12 18 24 36 48 54

SSID 3 : TLHMM
    Network type              : Infrastructure
    Authentication           : WPA2-Personal
    Encryption               : CCMP
    BSSID 1                  : 00:7f:28:bd:f8:15
        Signal               : 35%
        Radio type           : 802.11n
        Channel              : 6
        Basic rates  (Mbps)  : 1 2 5.5 11
        Other rates  (Mbps)  : 6 9 12 18 24 36 48 54

SSID 4 : PPP7C
    Network type              : Infrastructure
    Authentication           : Open
    Encryption               : WEP
    BSSID 1                  : 00:26:b8:63:3e:5c
        Signal               : 23%
        Radio type           : 802.11n
        Channel              : 6
        Basic rates  (Mbps)  : 1 2 5.5 11
        Other rates  (Mbps)  : 6 9 12 18 24 36 48 54

SSID 5 : CleverEagle
    Network type              : Infrastructure
    Authentication           : WPA2-Personal
    Encryption               : CCMP
    BSSID 1                  : 58:6d:8f:fa:75:90
        Signal               : 99%
        Radio type           : 802.11n
        Channel              : 2
        Basic rates  (Mbps)  : 1 2 5.5 11
        Other rates  (Mbps)  : 6 9 12 18 24 36 48 54

SSID 6 : Castellano
    Network type              : Infrastructure
    Authentication           : WPA-Personal
    Encryption               : TKIP
    BSSID 1                  : 00:14:bf:3b:2c:5c
        Signal               : 33%
        Radio type           : 802.11g
        Channel              : 6
        Basic rates  (Mbps)  : 1 2 5.5 11
        Other rates  (Mbps)  : 6 9 12 18 24 36 48 54

SSID 7 : FUKY3
    Network type              : Infrastructure
    Authentication           : Open
    Encryption               : WEP
    BSSID 1                  : 00:26:62:65:81:0c
        Signal               : 80%
        Radio type           : 802.11n
```

```
Channel          : 1
Basic rates (Mbps) : 1 2 5.5 11
Other rates (Mbps) : 6 9 12 18 24 36 48 54
```

What information is given for these available networks that is not given by the **show networks** argument? Which standards are represented in the output? You can use the example shown if the wlan context is not installed for netsh on your machine.

_____

_____

Lab 6.2 Review

1. Broadcast channels are an essential consideration in wireless devices. Any devices broadcasting on the same channel will have to share that channel for communication. Why would it be a bad idea for multiple wireless networks (owned and managed by different individuals or companies) to share a channel within the same broadcast radius? Use your textbook and Internet research to support your answer.

   _____

   _____

2. In wireless networking, the 802.11n standard is backward compatible with the 802.11g standard. Many 802.11n adapters are also backward compatible with the 802.11a and 802.11b standards. Similarly, the 802.11g standard is backward compatible with the 802.11b standard. Why is this important when choosing a wireless adapter and when connecting to a wireless network? What limitations are imposed by choosing a previous standard? Use your textbook and Internet research to support your answer.

   _____

   _____

   _____

   _____

Lab 6.3: WLAN Router Configuration

Approximate Lab Time: 15–20 min.
Prerequisite: Lab 6.2

Materials Needed: Paper/Pencil, PC Lab (Windows, USB Wireless Adapter, Cisco Linksys Router), Textbook, and Internet Research

This lab explores the setup of a wireless access point (AP), particularly a router that is designed to interface between wireless devices on the periphery of a network and the wired portion of the network (typically a LAN). You will explore the administrative management of a Cisco Linksys router and examine how APs relate to each other in a broadcast domain. As part of this lab, you will explore the communication paths within a wireless BSS and the limitation of connecting hosts that do not share the same domain. Compile a lab report of the solutions to the assigned exercises and include a review of the work necessary to arrive at the solution.

Wireless Routing

Modern wireless routers have an inherent setup utility that guides the user through the initial setup process. You can see an example of this in Figure 6-5. The router will typically choose its own broadcast channel. However, you can modify the access password and allow others to connect to the AP as guests.

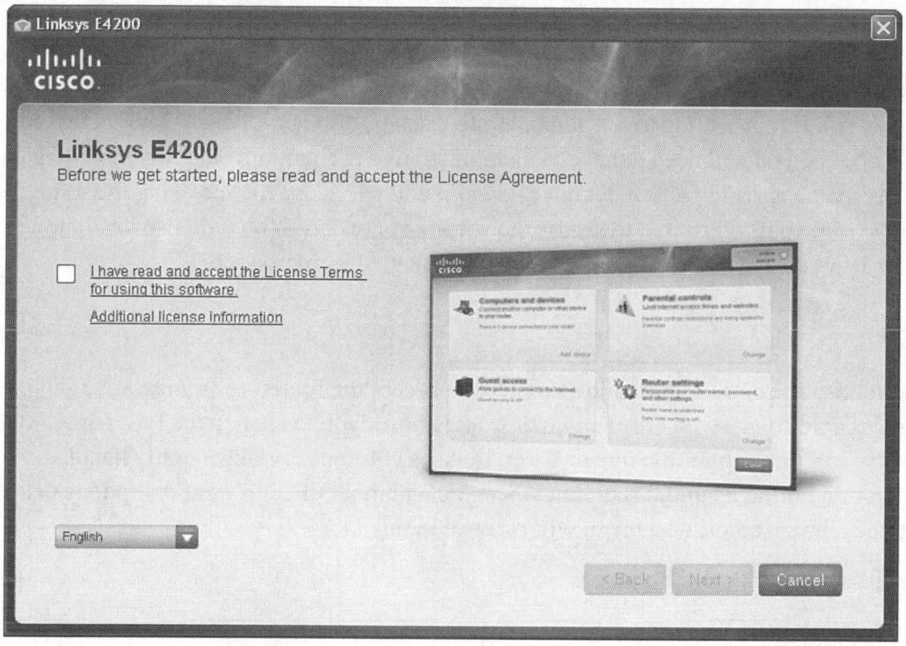

FIGURE 6-5   Initial Router Setup Example

Channel selection is one of the critical elements of routers. The channels in radio frequencies are spaced 5 MHz apart. These channels overlap in use, so they need to be spaced at least 25 MHz apart to function without interference. The recommended channels in the 2.4-GHz WLAN domain are 1, 6, and 11, though others can be used safely. Most routers are set to channel 6 by factory default. Newer routers have dynamic frequency selection (DFS) to allow them to choose a channel with less interference.

> **NOTE:** If your wireless router has not been set up, you should use the default settings and take note of the SSID and router password for future use. You will also need the router IP address and administrative username for this lab. If your router has been set up, you should get this information from your instructor.

Exercise 6.3.1

Choosing an SSID is another element in configuring a router for use. Why are SSIDs used instead of IP addresses or MAC addresses? Use your textbook and Internet research to support your answer.

_____

_____

_____

Configuring a Wireless Router

For this exercise, you will be connecting to the administrative setup for one of the wireless routers in your classroom. To do this, you will need to have the administrative account information, including the username (the username is set to factory default as *admin*) and password for accessing the router (this is commonly the same password used to access the wireless network). You will also need the IP address of the router itself so that you can access it directly through a web browser.

Exercise 6.3.2

For this lab, you will need to complete the following steps to access the router's administrative setup software. This is accessible from a web browser window and allows you to change the host name, guest access, security, and filtering for the router. Cisco Linksys equipment will generally handle most of the configuration during its initial setup, but there are a number of configuration options that can be changed by the administrator, which you will practice in this lab.

To access the wireless router, follow these steps:

STEP 1.   Open a web browser and enter the IP address of the wireless AP. When the connection is made, you should be prompted to enter a username and password. These are defined when you first set up the router. You can get these from your classroom facilitator if you do not have them. You can see an example of this prompt in Figure 6-6.

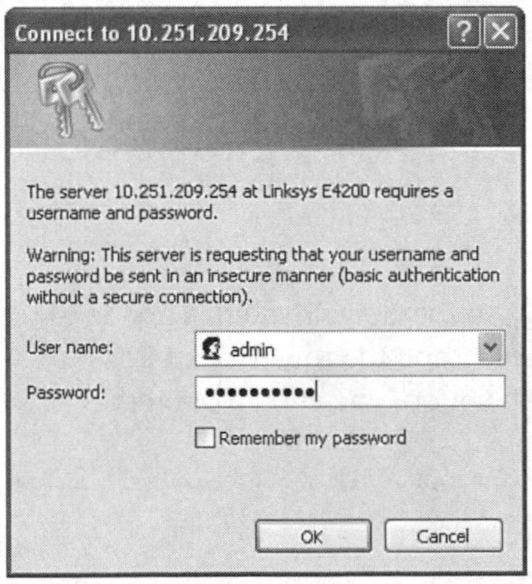

FIGURE 6-6   Wireless AP Credential Request

STEP 2. When you enter your credentials and click **OK**, you might get a warning screen showing that changing any of the configurations can cause the wireless AP to stop functioning correctly and can hinder the use of the Cisco Connect repair utility, as shown in Figure 6-7. You can ignore this, but you should not select the check box to make the warning disappear permanently.

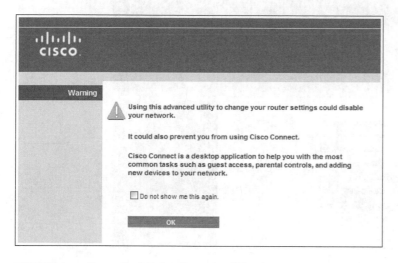

FIGURE 6-7   Example AP Configuration Warning

STEP 3. Click **OK** and you will be directed to the administrative software home page. This will be the basic setup page similar to what is shown in Figure 6-8. You can review the information and options you have available from this page, but you will not change any of the settings yet.

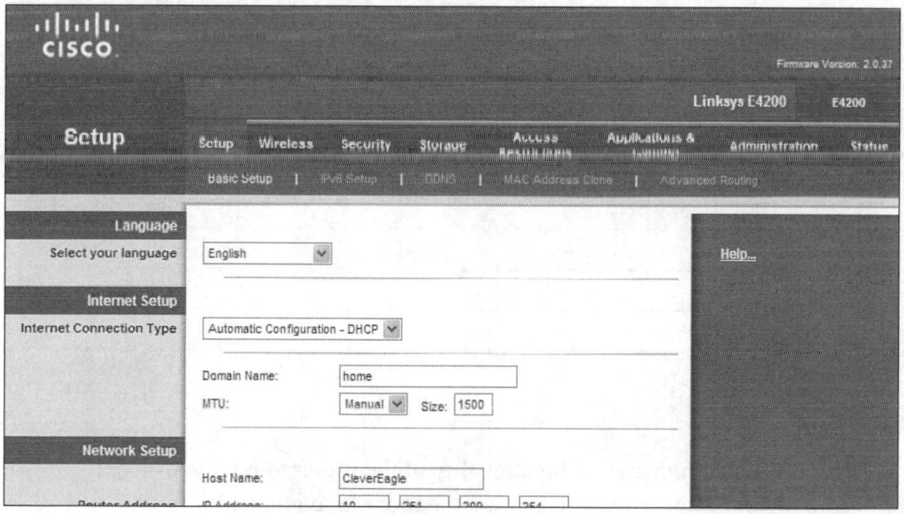

FIGURE 6-8   AP Software Home Page

STEP 4. Click the Status link in the upper-right corner. This will open a page displaying the current router information and the settings that are currently enabled, like the one shown in Figure 6-9. There are several links within the category of Status that can be explored, including the status for the local-area network and the wireless network.

FIGURE 6-9   Example AP Status Screen

Using the sublinks within the AP Status link, determine the MAC address for the AP on the LAN and the WLAN. Are these values the same? Why or why not? What IP address is used for the router on the WLAN? What addresses are available for the router to assign (under the DHCP settings; these will typically be based on the router's own settings)?

_____

_____

_____

_____

_____

_____

_____

_____

Exercise 6.3.3

For this exercise, you will use the administrative functionality of the router to ping your local machine. If you are unsure of your IP address, you can run the **ipconfig** command from the command-line interface to determine it. In the wireless router, click the Administration link and choose Diagnostics (this can vary slightly depending upon the router model). You can see an example of this in Figure 6-10.

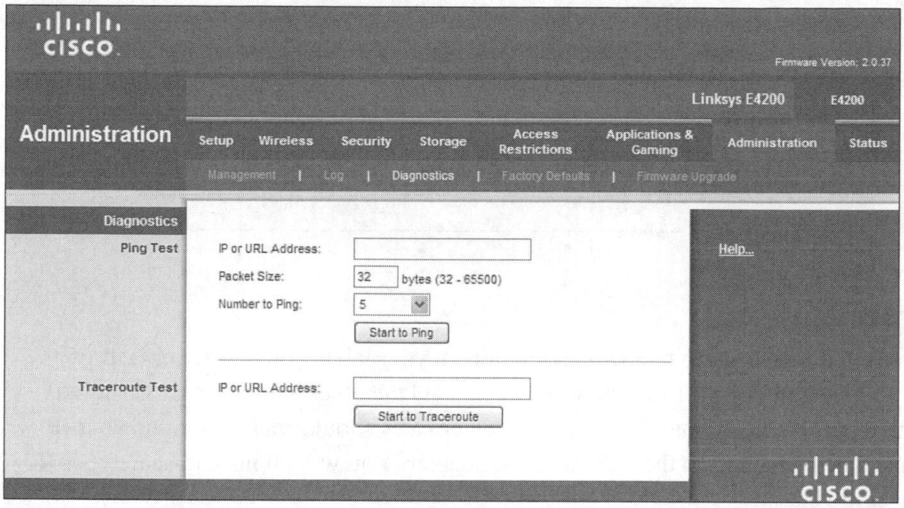

FIGURE 6-10   Example AP Administrative Tools

Use the diagnostic tools available to ping your machine. What other tools are available? How does this help you to determine connectivity issues on the network?

_____

_____

_____

Exercise 6.3.4

For this exercise, you will enable guest access on the AP. To allow this, you will click the Wireless link and choose Guest Access from the sublinks that appear. You can see an example of this in Figure 6-11. Choose **Yes** to allow guest access.

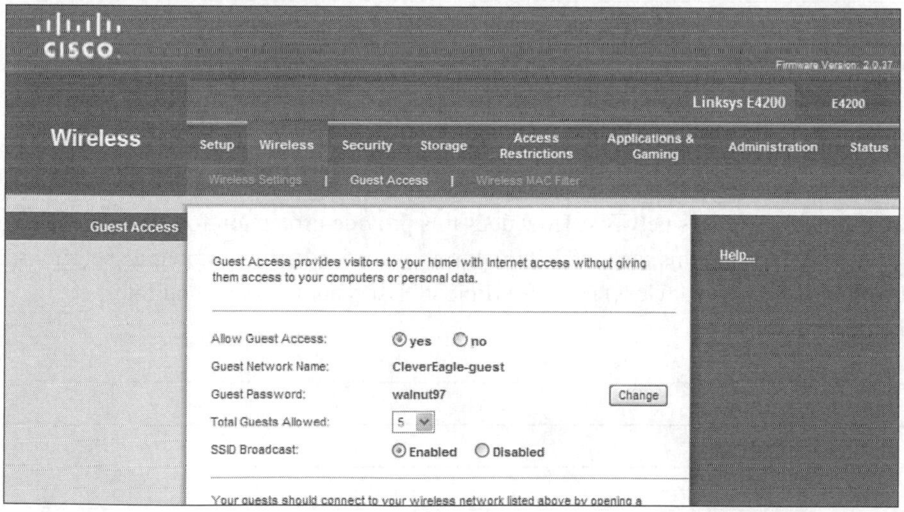

FIGURE 6-11   Example AP Status Screen

What is the SSID for the guest network? What other configuration options are available for modifying the guest network settings? What happens to the list of available wireless networks after you save the settings?

_____

_____

_____

Wireless Domains

You should be connected to one of the two wireless routers in your lab for this exercise. Half of the class should be connected to one of the wireless routers, and the other half of the class should be connected to the other wireless router. You and your classmates should each determine your IP addresses of the machine connected to the USB wireless adapter. You will all need to share your IP addresses with the entire class.

Exercise 6.3.5

Using the command-line interface, attempt to send a ping message to each of your classmates' IP addresses. Which of your classmates' machines responded to the ping? Which of them did not? What does this mean about the interconnectivity of wireless domains?

_____

_____

Lab 6.3 Review

1. What risks (if any) are posed by allowing guest access to your network? Use your textbook and Internet research to justify your answer.

_____

_____

_____

_____

2. MAC filtering on an AP allows you to set the MAC addresses of the devices that you will or will not allow to use the wireless network. How does this provide protection for your network? What is the drawback of using this feature? Which form of MAC filtering (allowing specific devices or disallowing specific devices) is more efficient? Use your textbook and Internet research to justify your answer.

_____

_____

_____

_____

_____

Lab 6.4: WLAN Placement

Approximate Lab Time: 15–20 min.
Prerequisite: Lab 6.1
Materials Needed: Paper/Pencil, Textbook, and Internet Research

This lab reviews the placement and capacity of wireless access points (AP). This includes the comparison of antenna types for wireless broadcasting. You will also decide which of these antennas to use and the channel to use for overlapping coverage of the APs in an Extended Service Set (ESS). Compile a lab report of the solutions to the assigned exercises and include a review of the work necessary to arrive at the solution.

Wireless AP Placement and Configuration

The placement of wireless devices to provide a continuous coverage area (in an ESS) requires careful planning for both the channel and the type of antenna used for each AP that needs to be included. For this lab, consider the network needs of a campus building that requires wireless coverage for students and researchers. The classroom capacity is 25 students and an instructor. The research labs only need ten connections. Each AP can handle a maximum of 50 connections, but it is advisable to have less than the maximum number in use. It is also advisable to limit the external access to the WLAN because of the private nature of some of the network traffic. The building plan and the AP locations are shown in Figure 6-12.

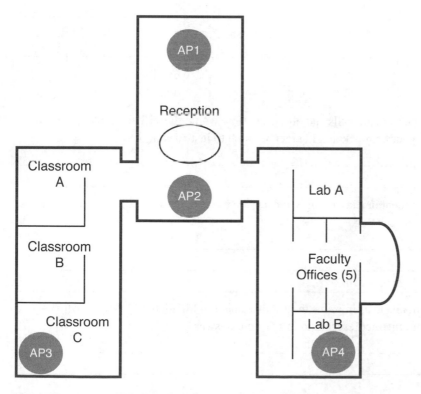

FIGURE 6-12   AP Placement in a Campus Building

Exercise 6.4.1

There are three main types of antennas that can be used for WLAN APs: directional, omnidirectional, and right-angle. Describe each of these antenna types. You can get more powerful antennas that can broadcast longer distances. Why would these antennas be limited in use for standard WLAN placement in a home?

_____

_____

_____

_____

_____

Exercise 6.4.2

Using Figure 6-12 as a guide, explain what type of antenna and which channel should be used for each of the APs that are placed. Given the capacity of each AP, is this placement sufficient to cover all the classrooms and labs? Why or why not?

_____

_____

_____

_____

_____

Lab 6.4 Review

1. Radio signals attenuate through walls and obstacles. How would this affect AP placement in a home or office? Use your textbook and Internet research to justify your answer.

_____

_____

2. To which AP will a student in Classroom B connect? What about a student in Classroom A? What about a student in Lab A?

_____

_____

_____

3. Would more powerful antennas improve the AP placement in Figure 6-12? Why or why not? Use your textbook and Internet research to justify your answer.

_____

_____

_____

_____

Chapter 7

Wide-Area Networks

This chapter will allow you to explore the concepts of wide-area networks (WAN). The primary distinction between WAN technology and the LAN technology explored in previous chapters is the transmission of data over long distances. In this chapter, you will explore the media and connection types used in WAN technology. You will also revisit command-line networking to explore communication paths to remote hosts. Finally, you will look at network examples and use WAN technologies to determine the best solution for connecting the locations. At the end of this chapter, you should be able to

- Identify the media used for connecting devices in a WAN
- Describe the common connection types and topologies for WANs
- Use Linux command-line networking to scan networks and identify remote pathways
- Plan optimal connection paths for networks that are separated by large distances

Lab 7.1: Distance Considerations

Approximate Lab Time: 15–20 min.

Materials Needed: Paper/Pencil, Textbook, and Internet Research

This lab reviews the challenges of communicating over large distances from LAN to LAN or from a remote point to an existing network. The media demands for this distance are higher than the requirements for transmission over the relatively short distance for LAN communication. However, you will find similar concepts and technologies in WAN communication to what is used in LAN communication. Compile a lab report of the solutions to the assigned exercises and include a review of the work necessary to arrive at the solution.

Crossing Distance with Signals

WAN connections are used to connect remote locations into a single network. An example of the type of distance for this connection would be from New York City to Orlando, Florida. You can consider the case where a business has locations in multiple cities, where each location needs a means to communicate with the other locations. LAN technologies are insufficient for this type of exchange and the land between the locations will not all be owned by the organization that wants to establish the connection.

Exercise 7.1.1

Part of the distinction between LAN and WAN networks is ownership. Why is it impractical for an organization to own the entirety of a WAN? Why is it favorable for an organization to maintain ownership of the entirety of a LAN? Use your textbook and Internet research to compose your answer.

_____

_____

_____

_____

Exercise 7.1.2

Given the problems with maintaining signals in short-range communications, what effect will increasing the required transmission distance have on transmitting the signal clearly?

_____

_____

Wide-Area Network Media

There are different types of media available for connecting devices over long distances, just as there are for connecting devices in local proximity. In fact, most of the media available for LAN technologies can be found in WAN connections as well. This is because WAN connections are typically not just a single long wire running from one end to the other but rather a path through a WAN infrastructure. Table 7-1 contains a partial list of physical media found in WANs.

Table 7-1   WAN Physical Media

Media	Infrastructure	Summary
UTP	Phone lines	
Coaxial	Television cable	
Fiber-optic		Uses a customized infrastructure to run dedicated connections; this is a costly option.
Electric power lines		This type of media can be used with Broadband over Power Lines (BPL), making use of the extensive infrastructure in place already.

Exercise 7.1.3

Complete Table 7-1 using your textbook and Internet research for support.

There is a greater variety of wireless technologies available for WAN connections than there is for LAN technologies. Most of these require specific configurations to detect and use. The wireless nature of these technologies saves on the infrastructure requirements for making connections over large distances, but they tend to be less reliable than physical infrastructure. A partial table of the available WAN wireless technologies is shown in Table 7-2.

Table 7-2   WAN Wireless Media

Media	Summary
Satellite	
WiMAX (Worldwide Interoperability for Microwave Access)	
HSPA+ (Evolved High-Speed Packet Access)	
Radio frequency	

Exercise 7.1.4

Complete Table 7-2 by providing a summary of the use of each wireless technology for creating WAN connections. Use your textbook and Internet research to compose your answer.

Lab 7.1 Review

1. How can cables like UTP and coaxial cable be used for long-distance communication in a WAN infrastructure? Where are these cables used most often? Use your textbook and Internet research to compose your answer.

_____

_____

_____

_____

2. Radio frequencies can be used for WLANs as well as for WAN connections. If the broadcast range can be increased for use in a WAN, why is the frequency and therefore broadcast radius limited for WLAN APs? Use your textbook and Internet research to compose your answer.

_____

_____

_____

_____

Lab 7.2: WAN Connections

Approximate Lab Time: 20–25 min.
Prerequisite: Lab 7.1

Materials Needed: Paper/Pencil, Textbook, and Internet Research

This lab reviews the different types of wide-area networks and the common topologies for WAN implementations. You will explore the concept of a dedicated leased line and the common standards and speeds available for this type of WAN link. Compile a lab report of the solutions to the assigned exercises and include a review of the work necessary to arrive at the solution.

WAN Connection Types

WAN links are expensive for point-to-point connections. There are a number of infrastructures already in place that minimize the cost, such as the telephone, cable, and power line infrastructures as well as the cellular infrastructure; these have all been adapted to support data transmission. When such infrastructure is not already present, new connections over large distances must be implemented. There are three such topologies that are common in WAN connections: dedicated leased lines, hub-and-spoke topologies, and partial/full-mesh connections.

Exercise 7.2.1

A dedicated leased line is one of the more expensive solutions to WAN connections, but it provides an always-on connection between two locations. This is incorporated into the local networks at both ends by adding a specialized router to each LAN. What are the benefits of using a dedicated leased line? What are the limitations of using a dedicated leased line?

_____

_____

_____

_____

Exercise 7.2.2

You should be familiar with mesh topologies from their use in LAN communications. In WAN technologies, the connections between sites are much more expensive (each of these can be a dedicated leased line itself). This type of topology is useful for decentralizing the different sites and creating multiple paths of communication in case one of the lines is down. A full mesh is often far too costly for deployment, but partial-mesh connections are more manageable. You can see an example of a partial-mesh connection in Figure 7-1.

> **NOTE:** Even though there are similarities in the structure of WAN and LAN topologies and even some common media in use, the physical and data link layer connections and transmission are very different between the two.

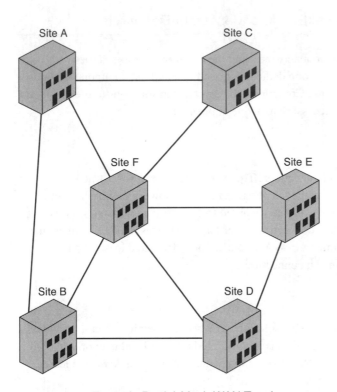

FIGURE 7-1   Example Partial-Mesh WAN Topology

What are the benefits of using a partial-mesh topology? When would a full-mesh topology be required? What is the difficulty in creating a full-mesh topology for sites in different geographical locations?

_____

_____

_____

_____

Exercise 7.2.3

When a network needs to span multiple locations across distances, a hub-and-spoke topology is often useful. This centralizes a single node of the network with individual links to the outlying locations. You can see an example of this type of network topology in Figure 7-2.

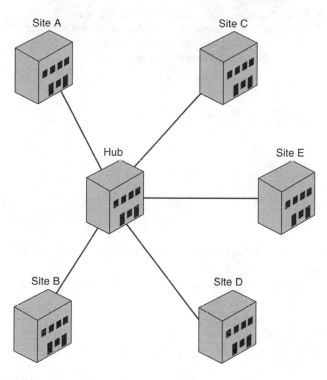

FIGURE 7-2   Example Hub-and-Spoke WAN Topology

What are the benefits of this type of topology over a partial-mesh or full-mesh connection over long distances? When would this topology be less desirable than a mesh solution?

_____

_____

_____

_____

_____

_____

_____

_____

Dedicated Leased-Line Connections

A dedicated leased line is one of the more expensive solutions for interconnecting two locations of LANs. This is often a good choice for businesses that need to interconnect separate locations for critical operations. These connections do not share bandwidth with any other subscribers, allocating all traffic to the two connected nodes. Table 7-3 presents a partial list of the common classifications for dedicated leased lines.

Table 7-3   Dedicated Leased-Line Classifications

Circuit Classification	Total Bandwidth (Mbps)	Features and Summary
T1	1.544	
E1		Uses 32 channels for communication (only 30 can transmit); transmits 16 frames at a time.
E3	34.4	
T3		

Exercise 7.2.4

Complete Table 7-3 using your textbook and Internet research, summarizing the features (such as the number of channels) available on the connection.

Lab 7.2 Review

1. The common Layer 2 protocol used on dedicated leased lines is the Point-to-Point Protocol (PPP). Use your textbook and Internet research to define PPP. Explain what a control protocol (CP) is and how it is used.

    _____

    _____

    _____

    _____

    _____

    _____

    _____

2. WAN connection speeds are often lower than modern LAN speeds. Explain why LANs need to handle more traffic than a WAN connection. What factors limit WAN technology but are less of a concern for LANs? Use your textbook and Internet research to justify your answer.

    _____

    _____

    _____

    _____

3. Another type of WAN technology is SONET. Use your textbook and the Internet to briefly define this type of WAN connection. What is the maximum available bandwidth on this type of network connection?

_____

_____

Lab 7.3: Communication Paths

Approximate Lab Time: 10–15 min.
Prerequisite: Lab 7.2
Materials Needed: Paper/Pencil, Textbook, and Internet Research

This lab explores the concept of communication paths in networking. Mapping these paths on a LAN is relatively straightforward, even for larger networks. However, when WAN connections are involved in a networking solution, it becomes more difficult to predict the connections between devices. As you continue to explore networking in the coming chapters, you will encounter more information about Internet connectivity, which has even more complex networking interactions than single WANs or WAN connections. This lab will guide you down the path of determining network connections and identifying when your communications are going outside a network boundary. Compile a lab report of the solutions to the assigned exercises and include a review of the work necessary to arrive at the solution.

Determining Communication Paths

As you have observed in wireless networking, two hosts must have a valid communication path to transmit information back and forth. This is true in wired communications as well, which present the additional problem of supporting infrastructure. Fortunately, there are a variety of technologies that can make use of existing infrastructure for creating new communication paths. In this lab, you will explore scenarios and analyze the connection paths between the parties that want to communicate.

Exercise 7.3.1

An organization needs to construct a WAN infrastructure for its supply chain across a state. The locations of each part of the organization are shown in Figure 7-3. Some of the communication paths are mission critical and others are not.

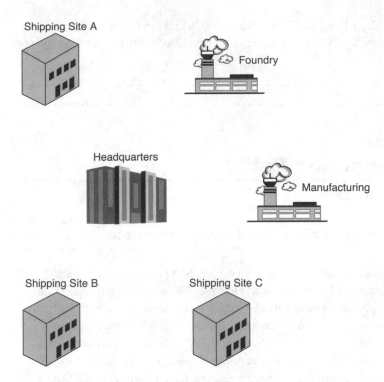

FIGURE 7-3   Network Nodes for a WAN

The organization has the following needs:

- The shipping sites need to have constant communication.
- The foundry must communicate with manufacturing with only limited downtime.
- Headquarters must be able to communicate with manufacturing to place orders daily.

Construct a diagram of the most effective structure for the organization's WAN connections and justify your choices.

Exercise 7.3.2

An organization needs to establish a connection between one of its locations in New York and another location in London, England. This means that the WAN connection must cross the Atlantic Ocean. Provide at least two options that are available for this organization to use. Use your textbook and Internet research to compose your answer. Which option would you suggest and why?

_____

_____

_____

_____

Lab 7.3 Review

1. One possibility for connecting two locations over a large distance is through the use of Virtual Private Networks over an Internet connection. Why is this type of network cost effective? What connectivity is required for both parties? Use your textbook and the Internet to research your answer.

   _____

   _____

   _____

2. What is the most efficient WAN topology for leased lines connecting five locations over distance if none of the connections are mission critical? What is the most effective topology if the communication path between any two sites is a high priority, where the probability of failure on any leased line is small (meaning that it is possible for it to fail but it is unlikely to fail)? Justify your answer.

   _____

   _____

   _____

   _____

   _____

   _____

Lab 7.4: Linux Networking

Approximate Lab Time: 20–25 min.
Prerequisite: Lab 6.3

Materials Needed: Paper/Pencil, PC Lab (Linux, USB Wireless Adapter), Textbook, and Internet Research

While you have already used some of the available commands for command-line networking in Windows, it is important to explore the available commands for Linux machines as well. Linux is commonly used as the OS for servers, and understanding the differences in the commands available in Linux versus Windows is essential for any networking professional. Now that you have studied WAN technology, you have a better understanding of routing paths, which you can use to explore the **traceroute** command further. Linux also has its own set of commands for wireless networking, which build upon your studies from Chapter 6, "Wireless LANs." Compile a lab report of the solutions to the assigned exercises and include a review of the work necessary to arrive at the solution.

Linux Command-Line Networking

The Linux networking commands are similar in structure and use to the Windows commands. With Linux, you can always learn more about the command and its available options using the man pages for the command (online or on the machine itself). For some of these exercises, you will need to bridge the connection to the host LAN with Internet access, and for others, you will need to bridge the USB wireless adapter. The network type is specified in each exercise.

Exercise 7.4.1

For this exercise, you will use the **ifconfig** command (similar to the **ipconfig** command in Windows) and the **arp**, **ping**, **traceroute** (spelled out instead of abbreviated as **tracert** in Windows), and **netstat** commands with which you are already somewhat familiar. You should bridge a connection to the LAN with Internet access for this exercise.

The **ifconfig** command is similar in use to the **ipconfig** command in Windows for gathering network connection information. Type the following command in the Linux terminal:

```
ifconfig
```

What information is given about the system?

_____

_____

The **arp** command in Linux will report the addresses for which a MAC address has been identified. Unlike Windows, the argument **-v** is used for the verbose version of **arp**. Run the following two commands in Linux:

```
arp
arp -v
```

What is the difference in the output of the two commands?

_____

The operation of ping is also different in Linux. By default, ping will run endlessly until the user presses **Ctrl+C** in the terminal window. You can control the number of ping messages sent with the argument **-c** and a number. You can test your local host access (whether the network interface is installed correctly) using the following command:

```
ping -c 4 localhost
```

What statistical information about the timing of the response is given as a summary after the ping messages are sent and returned?

_____

_____

The **traceroute** command in Linux is used to ping each hop in the path from the host machine to the identified host (by name or address). Use the **traceroute** command for two different web hosts (such as www.pearson.com and www.google.com) according to the following example:

```
traceroute www.google.com
```

Using your knowledge of LANs and WANs, which of the identified hosts and routers are part of the LAN network to which the host machine belongs? Which of the identified hosts and routers are part of the Internet service provider's WAN network for connecting to the Internet? How do you know when you have left the ISP WAN?

_____

_____

_____

The **ss** command in Linux is similar to the **netstat** command in Windows. It will return the current connection information for the host machine. Run the **ss** command (with no arguments or parameters) in your Linux machine terminal. What information does it return for each connection?

_____

_____

Exercise 7.4.2

For this exercise, you will use the **nslookup** commands in Linux. You should bridge the connection to the LAN with Internet access for this exercise. The **nslookup** command is used to gather host information for a host name or IP address. The format for the command is as follows:

```
nslookup 10.251.209.254
```

Run the **nslookup** command on your default gateway IP address. Run it again for an external web host (using the host name, such as www.google.com). What information is returned in each case and how do these differ?

_____

_____

Exercise 7.4.3

Now that you have an understanding of wireless networking and WLANs, you can use the USB wireless adapter connected to the Linux machine to test the **iwconfig** command. This is similar in nature to the **ifconfig** command, except it detects wireless devices and extensions. Run the **iwconfig** command (without arguments or parameters). What information is given about your wireless adapter?

_____

_____

Read the man page for **iwconfig**. What are some of the settings that you can change for the wireless connection using the options in the **iwconfig** command?

_____

_____

Lab 7.4 Review

1. The **arp** command in Linux can be used to add and remove routes for the ARP address cache. In Linux, you need the name of the interface (such as eth0 for most Ethernet LAN connections) and the IP and MAC addresses to add a static route with the **-s** argument. You need to know the interface and IP address to remove the route using the **-d** argument. What is the command to add IP address 10.11.12.13 with MAC address 00:AA:BB:CC:DD:EE to the ARP cache? What is the command to remove it?

   _____

   _____

2. The **ping** and **traceroute** commands can return similar information for an individual host. When is **ping** more useful and when is **traceroute** more useful? What is the limitation of **ping** for networking diagnostics? How can the two be used together for troubleshooting?

   _____

   _____

   _____

   _____

   _____

   _____

   _____

   _____

   _____

   _____

   _____

   _____

   _____

   _____

   _____

   _____

   _____

   _____

   _____

   _____

Chapter | 8

The Internet Protocol (IP)

The Internet Protocol is the most widely used protocol for modern network connectivity. It can be used in LANs, WANs, and WLANs to provide logical addressing and routing information. For this chapter, you will explore some of the aspects of IP and its addressing structure. You will also further your exploration of routing and router configuration to plan and implement routing for a small office/ home office (SOHO) network. This chapter correlates to the concepts and ideas presented in Chapter 8 of your *Introduction to Networking* textbook. At the end of this chapter, you should be able to

- Describe and identify IPv4 address classes and subnet masks
- Assign a static IP address for a network interface or adapter
- Read routing tables and use the **route** command
- Plan a small office/home office (SOHO) configuration and set the router for SOHO use

Lab 8.1: IP Addressing and Classes

Approximate Lab Time: 20–25 min.
Prerequisite: Lab 5.2

Materials Needed: Paper/Pencil, PC Lab (Windows), Textbook, and Internet Research

IP addresses are divided into classes. This allows an easy distinction between the number of hosts allowed on a single network. You can identify this quickly with the subnet mask used for the network, which you have seen in your earlier exploration of network interfaces and adapters, as well as practice with the command-line interface in both Windows and Linux. Compile a lab report of the solutions to the assigned exercises and include a review of the work necessary to arrive at the solution.

IPv4 Address Classes

IPv4 addresses are commonly just referred to as IP addresses, with the distinction made for IPv6 addresses that include the suffix *-v6* representing the version. Originally, IP addresses were divided into classes that would identify the network address and host address in the same value. IP addresses consist of 4 bytes of information, commonly represented by the decimal value of each byte separated by periods (or dots); this is known as the dotted-decimal notation. Each byte of an address is assigned a letter, as shown in Figure 8-1.

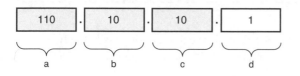

FIGURE 8-1 IP Address Example

Exercise 8.1.1

Class A networks are defined as those that use only the first byte (also called an octet) of the address as the network identifier. The rest of the address is considered the host identifier. In this type of network, the number of possible networks is much smaller than the number of hosts that can be connected to the same network. If the IP address in Figure 8-1 belongs to a class A network, what is the network ID and what is the host ID? What are the binary values of the host ID and the network ID? Hint: You should use decimal-to-binary conversion skills on each octet of the address separately and chain the bytes together for the answer.

_____

_____

_____

> **NOTE:** Another way to look at IPv4 address classes is to examine the leading bits (the leftmost bits in the first octet). A class A address begins with a leading 0, a class B address begins with a leading 10, and a class C address begins with a leading 110.

Exercise 8.1.2

Table 8-1 shows a partial listing of the standards for the common classes of addresses used in IPv4. This includes the number of available hosts and the number of available networks with each class of address.

Table 8-1   IPv4 Classes

Class	Range of First Byte (Octet) in Decimal	Network ID	Host ID	Possible Networks	Possible Hosts per Network
A	0–127	A	b.c.d		
B				2^{14}	2^{16}
C		a.b.c	D		

Use your textbook and the Internet to complete Table 8-1. Why is the number of possible networks for each class not equal to 2 raised to the power of the number of bits used for the network ID?

_____

_____

_____

Exercise 8.1.3

Would the IP address in Figure 8-1 be valid as a class C address? Why or why not? Justify your answer.

_____

_____

IPv4 Subnet Masks

IP address classes were useful, but they proved ineffective for scalability of networks. As more devices required IP addresses, a new system had to be developed to allow the use of IP addresses beyond the class limitations. The new scheme that was created was the classless interdomain routing (CIDR) system, which requires two values for determining a network ID and host ID, the IP address, and a subnet mask. A subnet mask has the same format as an IP address, but it uses 1s to identify the portion of the address allocated to the network ID and 0s to identify the portion of the address allocated to the host ID. You can see an example of this in Figure 8-2.

> **NOTE:** IP addresses that make use of a subnet mask are not subject to conformity to the class prefixes used in classful IP addressing. Subnet masks can have arbitrary lengths that do not conform to full octets being devoted to either the network ID or host ID.

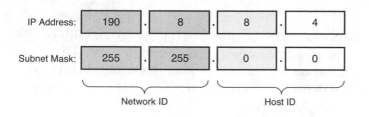

FIGURE 8-2 Subnet Masking in IPv4

Exercise 8.1.4

According to the subnet mask, what is the network ID of the IP address shown in Figure 8-2? What is the host ID of the IP address shown in Figure 8-2? What is the binary network ID? What is the binary host ID? Does this IP address conform to the rules of classful networking? Why or why not?

_____

_____

_____

_____

Exercise 8.1.5

There is a shorthand notation for subnet masks called slash notation to represent the subnet mask instead of using dotted-decimal notation. Another name for this slash notation is the classless interdomain routing (CIDR) notation. An example of this would be the address 190.8.8.4/16 for the address shown in Figure 8-2, where there are 16 1s in the subnet mask. $11111111_2 = 255$, so the mask for the network ID is 1111111111111111_2, which contains 16 1s.

What is the slash notation equivalent of subnet mask 255.255.255.0? What is the slash (or CIDR) notation equivalent of subnet mask 255.128.0.0? Show the work you used to derive your answer.

_____

_____

_____

Private Address Blocks

The Internet Assigned Numbers Authority (IANA) has reserved a number of addresses in each class as private. These addresses cannot be publicly routed over the Internet but are instead reserved for use on internal subnets, such as those that share a router where the router is the only connection to the Internet. Table 8-2 shows the IANA reserved private address blocks.

Table 8-2 IANA Reserved Private Address Blocks

Block Size	Starting IP Address	Ending IP Address	Subnet Mask (Slash Notation)
24-bit block	10.0.0.0	10.255.255.255	
20-bit block	172.16.0.0	172.31.255.255	
16-bit block	192.168.0.0	192.168.255.255	

Exercise 8.1.6

Complete Table 8-2 with the correct subnet mask for the private address blocks. To determine these values, convert the starting IP address to binary and the ending IP address to binary; next, count the number of bits that both addresses have in common. For example, $10.0.0.0 = 00001010.00000000.00000000.00000000_2$ and $10.255.255.255 = 00001010.11111111.11111111.11111111_2$; these have the first 8 bits in common, giving a subnet mask of 255.0.0.0.

Lab 8.1 Review

1. Use the **ipconfig** command on your Windows machine to identify the IP address and subnet mask used for your computer. What class of address is it? Are you able to identify it based on the first octet, by the subnet mask, or both? (If the subnet mask does not match the expected class from the IP address, choose the class based on the subnet mask.) Is your IP address part of the private address block?

   _____

   _____

   _____

   _____

   _____

   _____

2. Does the use of subnet masking invalidate any of the classful address assignments in IPv4, or does it expand the addressing capabilities while upholding the class rules for older addresses? Use your textbook and Internet research to justify your answer.

   _____

   _____

   _____

   _____

   _____

   _____

Lab 8.2: Assigning Static IP Addresses

Approximate Lab Time: 15–20 min.
Prerequisite: Lab 8.1

Materials Needed: Paper/Pencil, PC Lab (Windows), Textbook, and Internet Research

IP addresses can be assigned dynamically (typically through a DHCP host) or they can be assigned statically. When an IP address is assigned statically, it is no longer subject to DHCP configuration.

This can have a number of benefits for network configurations that are mostly stable. It is also required for remote hosts such as web servers to be consistently reachable through DNS resolution. Compile a lab report of the solutions to the assigned exercises and include a review of the work necessary to arrive at the solution.

Static IP Addressing

A unique IP address is necessary when a resource is connected directly to the Internet to allow traffic to find the correct host. The device may be a single machine or a representative of a connected LAN (such as a home router). Whenever the host is a named host being used for World Wide Web traffic (or any other Internet service), it is essential that the IP address be consistent so that the host can be identified through Domain Name System (DNS) resolution from any Internet-connected host. This is not the only use of static IP addresses, though. You can also assign them to local hosts within a network. In this lab, you will assign a static IP address to your machine.

Exercise 8.2.1

Complete the following steps to assign a static IP (IPv4) address to your PC. Be sure to record the values needed (especially for the default gateway) as you proceed.

STEP 1.   Use the command-line interface to run the **ipconfig** command. Record the default gateway's IP address. You will need to enter this value when you configure the static IP address.

STEP 2.   Open the Network Connections window within the Control Panel. Right-click the network adapter for which you want to assign a static IP address. Select **Properties** from the list, as shown in Figure 8-3.

FIGURE 8-3   Selecting Properties for a Network Adapter

STEP 3.   In the dialog box that opens, scroll to find the TCP/IP entry as shown in Figure 8-4. Click the **Properties** button.

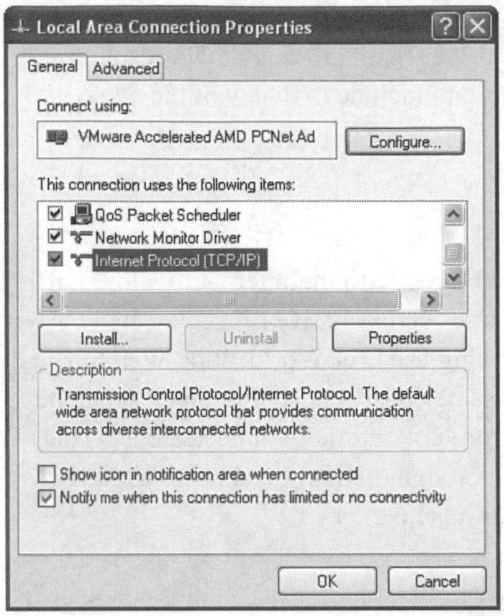

FIGURE 8-4   TCP/IP Entry in Connection Properties

STEP 4.   A new dialog box will open, Internet Protocol (TCP/IP) Properties, as shown in Figure 8-5. Choose the **Use the following IP address** option. Enter the static IP address, the subnet mask, and the valid entry for the default gateway. You should choose an IP address that resides on the same subnet as the default gateway (you can add 100 to the former IP address that was allocated dynamically).

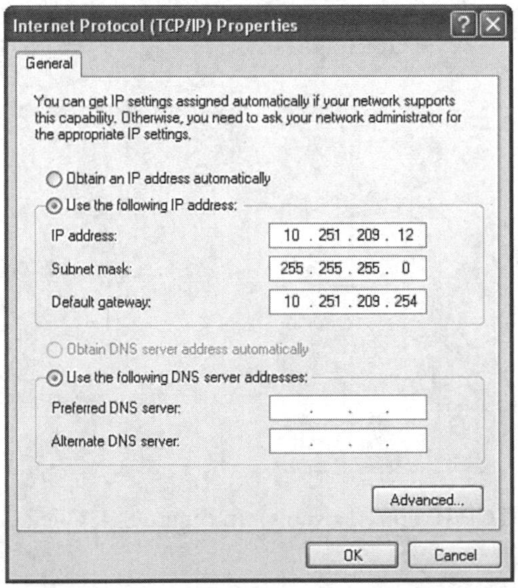

FIGURE 8-5   Subnet Masking in IPv4

STEP 5.   Click **OK** when you have finished entering the information. Then click **OK/Close** in the open Properties window. When this is complete, Windows will adjust your IP settings to the values you have entered.

STEP 6.   Go back to the command-line interface. Enter the **ipconfig** command to verify that the new settings have been implemented. Use the **ping** command to ping the default gateway and verify the connection.

> **NOTE:** Without a valid DNS server entry, the manual configuration will force Internet connectivity to use direct IP address connections only, disallowing names.

Use the process to enter an IP address that is not on the same subnetwork on which the default gateway resides. Does the **ipconfig** command still work? Does the **ping** command still reach the default gateway?

_____

_____

You should set your IP address back to automatic before moving on from this lab.

Lab 8.2 Review

1. How does the practice of assigning static IP addresses on a home or small office network make troubleshooting problems on the network easier? Use your textbook and Internet research to support your answer.

_____

_____

2. When would assigning static IP addresses be too cumbersome to be practical? What is the benefit of allowing hosts to dynamically acquire IP addresses through Dynamic Host Configuration Protocol (DHCP)?

_____

_____

_____

Lab 8.3: Routing Tables

Approximate Lab Time: 15–20 min.
Prerequisite: Lab 8.2

Materials Needed: Paper/Pencil, PC Lab (Windows), Textbook, and Internet Research

This lab reviews the logical routing tables maintained by a host machine. These are similar to the ARP tables maintained for physical addressing, determining the path that traffic should take to exit the network. You will practice reading the routing tables and managing the routes used by the host machine. Compile a lab report of the solutions to the assigned exercises and include a review of the work necessary to arrive at the solution.

Reading a Routing Table

The host machine maintains a network routing table similar to the ARP address cache. It defines the static IP routes on the machine as well as the dynamic configuration of addressing within the network, including the default gateway. You can access the routing table from the command-line interface with the following command:

```
route print
```

An example output from this command follows:

```
===========================================================================
Interface List
0x1 ........................ MS TCP Loopback interface
0x2 ...00 0c 29 a3 43 72 ...... VMware Accelerated AMD PCNet Adapter - Packet
Scheduler Miniport
===========================================================================
===========================================================================
Active Routes:
Network Destination        Netmask          Gateway       Interface  Metric
          0.0.0.0          0.0.0.0   10.251.209.254  10.251.209.132      10
     10.251.209.0    255.255.255.0   10.251.209.132  10.251.209.132      10
   10.251.209.132  255.255.255.255        127.0.0.1       127.0.0.1      10
   10.255.255.255  255.255.255.255   10.251.209.132  10.251.209.132      10
        127.0.0.0        255.0.0.0        127.0.0.1       127.0.0.1       1
        224.0.0.0        240.0.0.0   10.251.209.132  10.251.209.132      10
  255.255.255.255  255.255.255.255   10.251.209.132  10.251.209.132       1
Default Gateway:     10.251.209.254
===========================================================================
Persistent Routes:
  None
```

Exercise 8.3.1

The IP address destination entry 0.0.0.0 basically means "all traffic"—this address entry is used whenever there is no other specific route given. The Gateway entry here is the default gateway. The Interface entry represents the IP address of the network interface card (NIC) or adapter used as a source address. This should be your IP address. The host IP address should also appear in the list as a destination. The Gateway and Interface entry for this should be 127.0.0.1, which is the default "home" address of the machine.

What is the default gateway address in the example output? What is the machine's IP address and network mask? Copy and paste the output from the **route print** command on your own machine into your lab report.

_____

_____

_____

_____

Using the route Command

The **route** command has several arguments that allow you to manipulate the routing table for the host. These include **add** and **delete**. The following exercises will demonstrate the use of these arguments.

Exercise 8.3.2

You can use the **route** command to add a new route to the host machine. You must use a gateway that is on the local network. The format of this command is **route add** *destination gateway*. The destination can be any valid IP address. You can also optionally specify the network mask using the **mask** argument proceeded by the mask value. An example of the **route add** command follows:

```
route add 10.11.12.13 10.251.209.254
```

Using your default gateway, add a route to your system to connect to the IP address 10.11.12.13. What command did you use to enter the route? Run the **route print** command and paste the results into your lab report.

_____

_____

_____

Exercise 8.3.3

The command to delete the route is less complex than the command to add a route. To remove a route from the host's routing table, you only need the destination address. For example, to remove the route you added to 10.11.12.13, you would use the following command:

```
route delete 10.11.12.13
```

Run this command and confirm that the route has been removed by using the **route print** command. Practice adding a new route and removing it from the table. List the commands you used for this task.

_____

_____

_____

Lab 8.3 Review

1. The **route** command accepts the wildcard * (such as **route delete 10***, which deletes all routes beginning with the decimal value 10 regardless of the rest of the value). What are some possible uses of the wildcard value in determining or altering routes?

_____

_____

_____

_____

2. What would be the effect of deleting the route 0.0.0.0? Why would this be a problem for routing traffic?

_____

_____

_____

_____

_____

Lab 8.4: SOHO Planning

Approximate Lab Time: 15–20 min.

Materials Needed: Paper/Pencil, PC Lab (Windows, USB Wireless Adapter, Cisco Linksys Router), Textbook, and Internet Research

This lab represents a culmination of the previous chapters in which you will configure a router for small office/home office (SOHO) use. You will first plan the infrastructure and settings for the SOHO and then implement these on one of the wireless routers in the classroom. Compile a lab report of the solutions to the assigned exercises and include a review of the work necessary to arrive at the solution.

Planning a Home Network

Most home networks only require a single router because of the small number of devices connected to them and the shared connection to the Internet. As an example of this, consider the home shown in Figure 8-6. The potential locations for the wireless AP are shown in the figure as well. WLANs are ideal for home networking because they have no cable infrastructure associated.

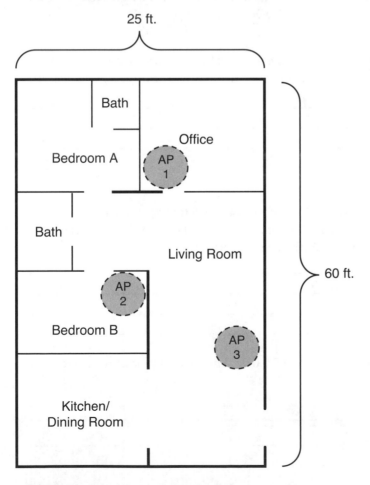

FIGURE 8-6   Example Home Layout

The thick interior lines mark load-bearing walls, which attenuate the wireless signal faster than the thin separation walls. The average wireless router can pass through three to four walls depending upon thickness. For this example, assume that the signal will attenuate when it passes through a load-bearing wall and any other wall or through two standard walls.

Exercise 8.4.1

Which of the three possible AP placement locations would work best to route to the entire home? Which location is least desirable? Justify your answer using your textbook and Internet research.

_____

_____

_____

_____

_____

_____

Exercise 8.4.2

If the home has three laptops, two Wi-Fi–enabled smart phones, two gaming systems, and a desktop PC in the office, is a single AP sufficient for routing the home network? Justify your answer.

_____

_____

_____

_____

SOHO Router Information

Now that you have a basic understanding of router setup, you can explore the additional features of the router and see how it can be configured for use in a home network or SOHO setting. Log in to the administrative pages of your Cisco Linksys router. You can do this by opening the router's IP address in a web browser and entering the username and password for the router configuration. The basic setup is already configured for the AP, which would allow it to run on most home networks and accept connections. Now that you are familiar with routing tables, you can start to examine some of the router properties more closely.

> **NOTE:** You should not change the host name, IP address, or password for the router, or you will disable access to it for your classmates!

Exercise 8.4.3

Access the routing table for the router. You can do this by clicking the **Setup** link and choosing the **Advanced Routing** sublink. You can then click the **Show Routing Table** button, as shown in Figure 8-7.

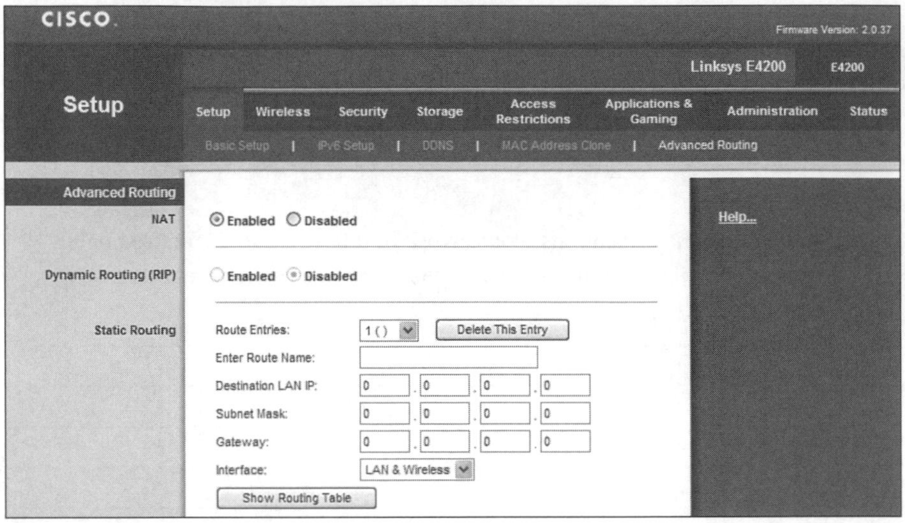

FIGURE 8-7 Example Advanced Routing Page on an AP

This will open a new window with the routing table entries, such as the one shown in Figure 8-8.

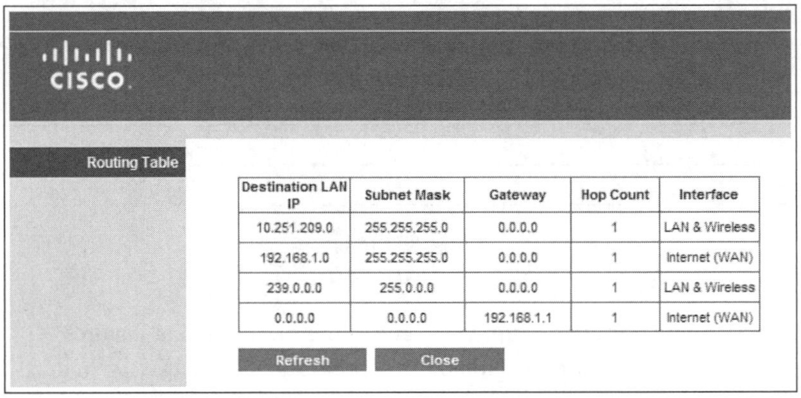

Destination LAN IP	Subnet Mask	Gateway	Hop Count	Interface
10.251.209.0	255.255.255.0	0.0.0.0	1	LAN & Wireless
192.168.1.0	255.255.255.0	0.0.0.0	1	Internet (WAN)
239.0.0.0	255.0.0.0	0.0.0.0	1	LAN & Wireless
0.0.0.0	0.0.0.0	192.168.1.1	1	Internet (WAN)

FIGURE 8-8 Example Routing Table from an AP

What do you notice about the gateway IP for most of the entries? What is the default gateway for the router? If there is no default gateway given in your router, use the example in Figure 8-8.

Exercise 8.4.4

Click the **Administration** link and select the **Log** sublink. Enable the activity log for the router. What kind of information or activity does the log display? How would this information be useful for monitoring or troubleshooting a home network?

_____

_____

_____

_____

Lab 8.4 Review

1. MAC address filtering can be enabled on most routers for home use, but this is not as useful or convenient as it is for office networks. How would this filtering be beneficial in a home environment? How would it be limiting for a home network to have this in place? Use your textbook and the Internet to justify your answer.

_____

_____

_____

_____

_____

2. Most routers have the capability to enable access restrictions (also called parental controls); this allows you to limit device access to the Internet or limit certain sites from being accessed. How would this functionality be useful for an office network?

_____

_____

_____

_____

_____

Chapter | 9

The Internet

The Internet is a global interconnection of networks, allowing any machine connected to it to reach any other connected host in the world. This chapter explores the different infrastructures for providing connectivity to the Internet. As part of this chapter, you will also look at the interconnectivity of subnetworks (subnets) and see how they can connect to the Internet individually or through a proxy server. This chapter correlates to the concepts and ideas presented in Chapter 9 of your *Introduction to Networking* textbook, including the need for a new addressing scheme as the IPv4 addresses are exhausted. At the end of this chapter, you should be able to

- Describe broadband Internet connections and understand how they function
- Identify subnets and hosts within the same network
- Describe IPv6 addressing and identify the need for IPv6 addresses
- Configure an FTP service for Internet use

Lab 9.1: Broadband Internet

Approximate Lab Time: 15–20 min.

Materials Needed: Paper/Pencil, Textbook, and Internet Research

Internet service providers (ISP) use a variety of infrastructures to provide Internet connectivity to homes and offices at varying speeds. This lab reviews the basic infrastructure and media types used by ISPs for providing broadband Internet connections. You will also explore the common types of digital subscriber lines (DSL) available. Compile a lab report of the solutions to the assigned exercises and include a review of the work necessary to arrive at the solution.

Broadband Connections

Internet service providers (ISP) use an existing infrastructure to allow end users to connect to the Internet. These ISPs began with the use of the existing telephone infrastructure to allow dialup connections to the Internet. The speed of these connections was limited, so new technologies were adopted to allow higher speeds over the infrastructure and an expansion to other types of infrastructure, such as coaxial (and sometimes fiber) television cable and even power lines.

Exercise 9.1.1

The original dialup connections offered by telephone companies required complete use of the telephone cable to connect to the Internet (meaning that no calls could be placed or received during the Internet connection). Why is this inefficient for establishing a connection to the Internet? What was the limitation of the data rates available on this type of Internet connection?

_____

_____

_____

_____

Exercise 9.1.2

The term _broadband Internet_ generally refers to higher-speed and constantly available connections to the Internet. The term represents an evolution of Internet connectivity, but it originally referred to the type of media usage. Broadband and baseband are the two types of media usage available. Briefly define these terms and explain the difference between them.

_____

_____

_____

_____

DSL Types

The digital subscriber line (DSL) represents the evolution of the original dialup connections for telephone access to the Internet. This allows the concurrent use of the telephone service and the Internet connection and provides faster speeds for the Internet connection. The DSL connections are limited by distance from the corporate headquarters. Some of the DSL types are shown in Table 9-1.

Table 9-1   DSL Connections Types

DSL Type	Description	Maximum Download Speed	Maximum Upload Speed	Maximum Distance (m)
Asymmetric DSL (ADSL) – ADSL2+	This has a much higher download speed than upload speed based on traffic statistics.	24 Mbps	1.4 Mbps	6000+
High-bit-rate DSL (HDSL)	This is comparable in performance to a T1 line; it has the same upload and download rate but requires two lines.			
ISDN DSL (IDSL)	This type of DSL operates at a fixed rate for both upload and download; it is primarily for users of Integrated Services Digital Network (ISDN).		144 Kbps	10,700

Table 9-1   continued

DSL Type	Description	Maximum Download Speed	Maximum Upload Speed	Maximum Distance (m)
Multirate Symmetric DSL (MSDSL)	This is a symmetric DSL type that is capable of more than one transfer rate.			
Rate Adaptive DSL (RADSL)	This is an asynchronous DSL type that can adjust speeds based on the length and quality of the connection line.			
Symmetric DSL (SDSL)	This type of DSL sends and receives data at the same rate.	2.048 Mbps	2.048 Mbps	3000
Very high-bit-rate DSL (VDSL) – VDSL2	This is a very fast asynchronous DSL that can only operate over short distances.			1000+

Exercise 9.1.3

Using your textbook and Internet research, complete Table 9-1 with the upload (outgoing) speed and download (incoming) speed as well as the maximum distance allowed between the end connection and the headquarters location.

Lab 9.1 Review

1. The cable television infrastructure has been incorporating fiber-optic cable since the 1990s into a hybrid fiber-coaxial (HFC) network. How does this type of network operate, and how does it act to extend the distance over which the signals can travel? Use your textbook and Internet research to compose your answer.

_____

_____

_____

_____

2. An emerging technology is Broadband over Power Lines (BPL), which can allow a host computer to access the Internet simply by plugging it into an electrical outlet. Use the Internet to research this technology and provide a brief description of this technology and its potential for adoption. Why does it pose a threat to other broadband service providers?

_____

_____

_____

_____

_____

_____

_____

Lab 9.2: Networks and Subnets

Approximate Lab Time: 25–30 min.
Prerequisite: Lab 1.3, Lab 8.1

Materials Needed: Paper/Pencil, Textbook, and Internet Research

This lab builds upon the foundations you have learned in network interconnectivity and IPv4 addresses with subnet masks. You will explore the reserved network host IDs within the host block and explore why a router will not communicate with a local machine whose IP address is not on the same logical network. You will also use the binary AND operation to determine which computers are on the same subnetwork based on their IP addresses and subnet masks. This is incredibly useful for determining network boundaries from traceroute results and packet captures. Compile a lab report of the solutions to the assigned exercises and include a review of the work necessary to arrive at the solution.

Calculating the Number of Hosts in a Given Network

The Layer 3 IP protocol is responsible for logical addressing and routing. This includes crossing network boundaries and identifying hosts within a given subnetwork (or subnet). Whenever you have an Internet-enabled router, you are sending traffic past the local network to another network, which passes the traffic farther until it reaches the network containing the Internet-enabled host you are trying to reach. The interoperability of IP networks is what allows the Internet to function. In this lab, you will explore the reserved host IDs in an address block and determine how many hosts can reside on a network based on the host ID.

Exercise 9.2.1

The number of bits available for the host ID on a network determines the number of hosts allowed to be connected to that network. For example, if you had 4 bits for the host ID, how many unique combinations can be made from 4 bits? Hint: Counting the numbers from 0000 to 1111 will give you all the possible combinations. What is another way to express this value as a power of 2? Hint: Each bit has two possible values.

_____

_____

_____

_____

Exercise 9.2.2

Using the formula for the number of available host ID values based on the number of bits you have for the host ID, answer the following questions. If you have a /24 network, how many unique host ID values exist? If you have a /16 network, how many unique host ID values exist (expressed as a number of a power of 2)?

_____

_____

_____

_____

The first reserved host ID is the network address, which uses all 0s for the host ID. This address cannot be used to identify a single host in the network. The next reserved address is the broadcast ID for the network, which uses all 1s as the host ID; this type of traffic will go to all hosts on the network.

Exercise 9.2.3

Given the dotted-decimal network ID prefix of 176.33.4 and subnet mask 255.255.255.0, what is the reserved network address? What is the reserved broadcast address? What is the first available host ID for a unique host on this network? What is the last available host ID for a unique host on this network? How many unique host addresses can be allocated on this network? Hint: Consider the actual addresses for the reserved network address and the reserved broadcast address; the available values are the range between these addresses.

_____

_____

_____

_____

Determining Whether Computers Are on the Same Logical Network

For devices to communicate over the local network, they must share a network ID. As you observed in Lab 8.2, when you change the IP address of a host so that it is no longer on the same network as the default gateway, the host cannot establish a communication path to the default gateway. This is because of the behavior of the gateway. The gateway receives the traffic locally, but when the gateway identifies the IP address as being outside the local network, the gateway passes the traffic through the network boundary, sending the traffic through the gateway's default connection for external traffic. The host therefore never receives the response from the gateway it attempted to contact. In situations like this, it is important to be able to determine whether two nodes reside within the same network boundary. This lab explores how you can use the IP addresses and subnet masks to determine whether two hosts are within the same network boundary.

> **NOTE:** Remember that the AND operation produces a 1 result only if both of its inputs are 1; otherwise, it will produce a 0 value.

To determine the network ID for any given IPv4 network, you can AND the binary IP address and its equivalent binary subnet mask. This becomes a clear method for quickly determining whether two hosts share a network (which only occurs when the resulting network ID matches). You can see an example of this in Figure 9-1.

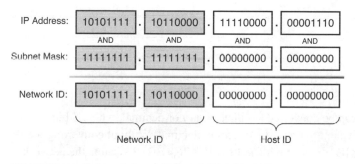

FIGURE 9-1   Determining a Network ID with AND

Exercise 9.2.4

Does the IP address 175.176.128.4 with subnet mask 255.255.0.0 reside on the same network as the example host in Figure 9-1? Why or why not?

_____

_____

_____

_____

Converting the address to binary as an intermediate step is not the most efficient way to determine the network ID. Instead, you can use the decimal subnet mask to predict the network ID quickly when the subnet mask is divisible by 8 (meaning that it uses complete octets for the network ID and the host ID). Whenever the subnet mask contains an octet of 255, this is equivalent to all 1s, meaning that octet from the IP address is part of the network ID. When the subnet mask contains an octet of 0, that part of the IP address will become 0 and represents part of the host ID. You can see an example of this in Figure 9-2.

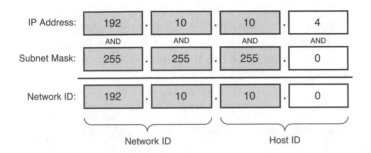

FIGURE 9-2   Determining a Network ID from the Subnet Mask

Exercise 9.2.5

Does the host with IP address 192.10.10.234 and subnet mask 255.255.255.0 reside on the same network as the host in Figure 9-2? Why or why not?

_____

_____

_____

Exercise 9.2.6

The slash notation for a subnet mask can be converted to either binary or decimal, where 8 bits of the subnet mask in slash notation are equivalent to one octet of 255 in decimal. Without converting the IP address to binary, what is the network ID of a host with address 173.76.4.3/16? What is the network ID of a host with address 126.35.77.4/24? Does the address 126.35.78.3/24 share a network with 126.35.77.4/24? Why or why not?

_____

_____

_____

_____

Lab 9.2 Review

1. How can you modify the formula for determining the number of unique host IDs available in a network to exclude the reserved network address and the reserved broadcast address? Explain your answer.

   _____

   _____

2. Can two hosts share a network if the number of 1s in the subnet mask for each of the hosts is different? Does this help you determine whether two hosts reside on the same network? Justify your answer.

   _____

   _____

   _____

   _____

Lab 9.3: Internet Protocol Version 6 (IPv6)

Approximate Lab Time: 15–20 min.
Prerequisite: Lab 8.1
Materials Needed: Paper/Pencil, Textbook, and Internet Research

Even with the addition of subnet masking and conservation efforts, the IPv4 address pool is not sufficient to uniquely address every Internet-connected device around the world. Because the IPv4 address pool was not sufficient, a new addressing scheme had to be created. The solution to this problem was the IPv6 address format, which can accommodate a much greater number of devices. This lab explores the structure and application of an IPv6 address. Compile a lab report of the solutions to the assigned exercises and include a review of the work necessary to arrive at the solution.

IPv6 Addressing

With the exhaustion of the available IPv4 addresses, a new version of the Internet Protocol was developed to solve the problem: version 6. The new address format for IPv6 uses 128 bits instead of 32 bits to represent a unique address. This uses 16 bytes of address space (each byte is called an octet in representation). IPv6 addresses are represented in hexadecimal characters rather than the decimal characters used for IPv4 addresses. You can see an example of an IPv6 address in Figure 9-3.

> **NOTE:** Whenever you see less than four characters in an IPv6 address segment, you can assume that leading 0s occupy the space to the left to pad the given value to four hexadecimal characters.

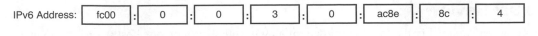

FIGURE 9-3   Example IPv6 Address

Exercise 9.3.1

What is the binary equivalent of the IPv6 address shown in Figure 9-3? How many bits are used for the address?

_____

_____

_____

_____

_____

_____

Like IPv4, there is a slash notation defining the network mask. The number behind the slash is equivalent to that number of 1s in the mask starting at the beginning of the address. This can also be represented in hexadecimal, where the letter $f_{16} = 1111_2$. You can see an example of this in Figure 9-4 using a hexadecimal representation of the subnet mask for ease of reading.

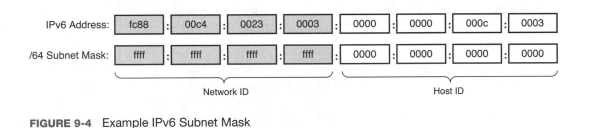

FIGURE 9-4   Example IPv6 Subnet Mask

Exercise 9.3.2

If the address in Figure 9-3 used a /56 mask, what would the network ID of the address be (in binary)? What would the host ID of the address be?

_____

_____

_____

_____

Configuring IPv6 on a Network Connection

For this lab, you will be using your Windows PC to install and configure an IPv6 address for your bridged LAN connection. Open the Network Connections window from within the Control Panel and be sure to have a network connection available (preferably a bridged connection to an Internet-enabled host).

Exercise 9.3.3

Complete the following steps to install IPv6 for your network connection:

STEP 1. Right-click the network connection you want to configure and choose **Properties**. A new dialog box should open.

STEP 2. Scroll down to TCP/IP in the list of items for the connection, as shown in Figure 9-5. After this item is selected, click **Install**.

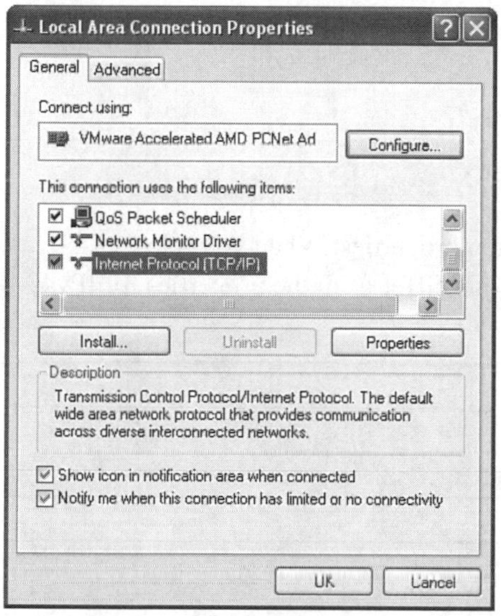

FIGURE 9-5   TCP/IP Selection in Network Connection Properties Dialog Box

STEP 3. This will open a new dialog box, where you will select the type of item to install. Choose **Protocol**, as shown in Figure 9-6. Then click **Add**.

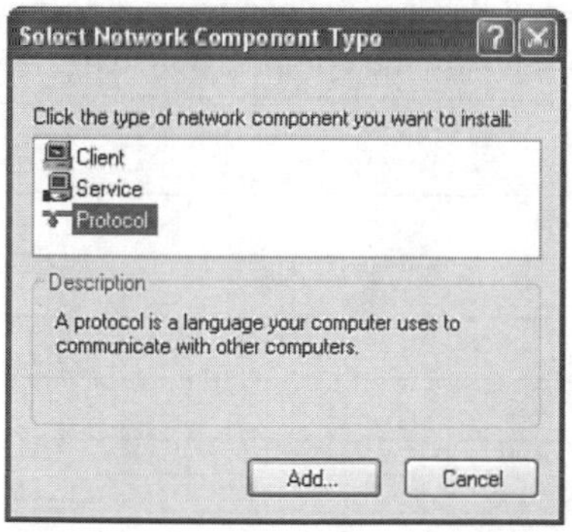

FIGURE 9-6   Protocol Selection in Component Type Dialog Box

STEP 4. In the new dialog box that opens, select **Microsoft TCP/IP version 6**, as shown in Figure 9-7. Then click **OK**.

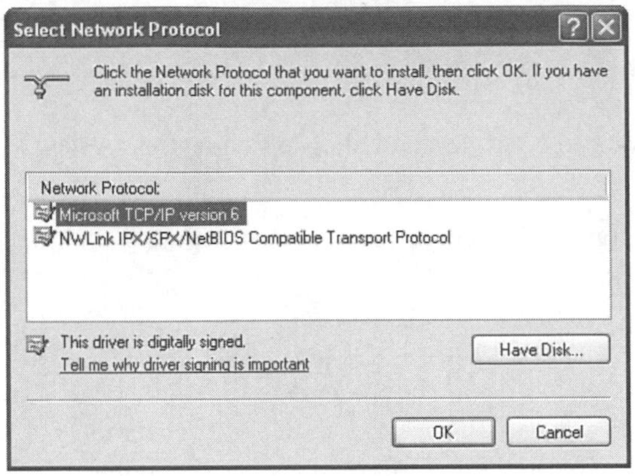

FIGURE 9-7   Protocol Selection in Component Type Dialog Box

The protocol should now appear in the items for the connection properties. When you select **Properties**, what options are you given for IPv6? How does this differ from the properties for IPv4?

_____

_____

_____

_____

_____

Lab 9.3 Review

1. It is possible to perform a single compression on an IPv6 address to shorten its display, where a string of 0 values is represented by a double colon. This is only possible when you have a consecutive string of 0 values for multiple segments of an IPv6 address. For example, the address fc77:0:0:0:3:0:0:4 could be abbreviated either as fc77::3:0:0:4 or fc77:0:0:0:3::4. Why can this notation only be used to compress one string of 0 values? What is the compressed form of the address in Figure 9-3? How many 0 values have been hidden by the compression? Use Internet research to compose your answer.

_____

_____

_____

_____

_____

_____

2. The IPv6 address block fe80::/10 is reserved for local network use. The MAC address of the NIC or adapter occupies the last 64 bits of this type of IPv6 addressing. How does this guarantee uniqueness for each device connected on an IPv6 local network?

_____

_____

_____

Lab 9.4: Configuring an FTP Service

Approximate Lab Time: 15–20 min.
Prerequisite: Lab 6.3

Materials Needed: Paper/Pencil, PC Lab (Windows, USB Wireless Adapter, Cisco Linksys Router), Textbook, and Internet Research

In addition to web pages, email, and the ability to globally interconnect hosts, one of the services provided by the Internet is the ability to transfer files remotely across network boundaries. The protocol that governs this type of transfer is File Transfer Protocol (FTP). Most Internet-enabled routers have the ability to establish an FTP service that can be linked to an IP address for remote access. In this lab, you will use the router in your classroom to configure this service. Compile a lab report of the solutions to the assigned exercises and include a review of the work necessary to arrive at the solution.

Configuring FTP on a Router

For this lab, you should connect your wireless adapter to your Windows virtual machine and connect to the assigned wireless router. Open the web interface for configuring the router remotely (by entering the IP address in the address bar of the browser) and sign in to the administration pages.

Exercise 9.4.1

For this exercise, you will enable and configure the FTP service available from your router. Complete the steps and be sure to answer any questions asked throughout the process as well.

> **NOTE:** Only one person at a time can configure this information on the router. You should record the settings you change and make sure to change them back for the next person if others are sharing the resource.

STEP 1. Log in to the administration pages for your wireless router.

STEP 2. Click the **Storage** link along the top navigation and click the **FTP Server** sublink that appears. This should open the main configuration window for starting the FTP service from the router. This service allows you to access a shared disk either internally on the local network or remotely using the Internet-routable IP address for the router. You can see an example of this page in Figure 9-8.

FIGURE 9-8   FTP Configuration Page for the Cisco Linksys E4200 Router

STEP 3.   You must first enable the FTP server and provide a name for the FTP server. The default port for FTP is 21 and the default encoding is Unicode (UTF-8, with which you should be familiar). To enable these changes and start the service, you must choose at least one folder to share. This is possible only if you have an external memory disk attached to your router. If you do have this, you can click the **Specify Folder** button to configure it. Otherwise, just record the settings you chose for this service.

You also have the ability to allow Anonymous FTP, which would allow read-only access to your folder from users who do not provide credentials for the FTP site. When would this be beneficial? When would you want this access to be disabled? Use Internet research to justify your answer.

_____

_____

_____

_____

_____

_____

_____

Lab 9.4 Review

1. What is the benefit of having FTP service available on a router? Consider SOHO configurations in your answer. Use your textbook and Internet research to compose your answer.

_____

_____

_____

_____

_____

2. When would you want FTP service configured only for the local network and when would you want it configured for Internet use? Use your textbook and Internet research to compose your answer.

_____

_____

_____

_____

_____

_____

_____

_____

_____

_____

_____

_____

_____

_____

_____

_____

_____

Chapter | 10

TCP/IP Transport

This chapter covers the layers of interconnectivity above routing, such as the TCP protocol used for World Wide Web communication. As part of this chapter, you will explore the ports used by common Layer 4 communication protocols over the Layer 3 routing. You will also examine the common network management protocol SNMP. As a final exercise, you will take a detailed look at the network traffic used in communication between a host and a website. This chapter correlates to the concepts and ideas presented in Chapter 10 of your *Introduction to Networking* textbook. At the end of this chapter, you should be able to

- Describe the common transport layer protocols
- Identify the common ports in use in network communications
- Describe the Simple Network Management Protocol (SNMP) and understand how it operates
- Perform a packet capture for identifying the traffic and protocols used for connecting from a host to the World Wide Web

Lab 10.1: Transport Layer Networking Protocols

Approximate Lab Time: 15–20 min.

Materials Needed: Paper/Pencil, Textbook, and Internet Research

The transport layer (Layer 4 of the OSI model) is responsible for establishing connections between hosts on a network. While the routing actually takes place at Layer 3 (the network layer of the OSI model), the transport layer identifies the sender to the recipient and provides a means of response, whether a session is established between the two hosts or not. The two most common transport layer protocols in use are the Transport Control Protocol (TCP) and the User Datagram Protocol (UDP). You have encountered these briefly already, but this lab will explore each of these protocols and their functionality in greater depth. Compile a lab report of the solutions to the assigned exercises and include a review of the work necessary to arrive at the solution.

Transport Control Protocol (TCP)

TCP is one of the two common OSI Layer 4 (transport Layer) protocols in use on Internet and IP networks. At the transport layer, the source and destination are identified by software port numbers instead of IP addresses. These addresses are indicated in common use by a colon following the IP address with the assigned port number, so for a host with IP address 172.43.7.4, port 80 would be identified as 172.43.7.4:80. The source and destination ports do not have to be the same.

Exercise 10.1.1

TCP can connect two hosts with the capability to retransmit dropped packets, maintain ordering, and check for errors. A TCP connection is established with a three-way handshake in which a connection is established and acknowledged. What are the three messages that form this handshake sequence? Why is this important for establishing the connection? Use your textbook and Internet research to compose your answer.

_____

_____

_____

_____

Exercise 10.1.2

By establishing a TCP connection, you allow one host to verify expected communication to and from the connected host. This provides two important features: windowing/sequencing and error checking/recovery. Windowing and sequencing are used to determine whether messages have been seen and are delivered in the correct order to the recipient. Error checking makes sure that all the packets are delivered as expected, providing reliability. Why are reliability and sequencing important in message delivery? Give an example of when each would be necessary.

_____

_____

_____

_____

_____

User Datagram Protocol (UDP)

TCP provides reliability and message ordering, but it requires network overhead (the use of network resources for management rather than data transmission). In contrast to this, the UDP protocol does not provide any of these services, but it has almost no associated overhead. The UDP header is only 8 bytes in length compared to the 20 bytes of the TCP header. UDP includes only the source port, destination port, length, and checksum (all of which are included in the TCP header as well as a number of other fields). UDP is a lightweight protocol that does not allow handshake connections; it is used to send a message without response or acknowledgment.

Exercise 10.1.3

What type of messages can be sent without confirmation or acknowledgment? Why is it useful to have a protocol that operates like this?

_____

_____

Table 10-1 presents a partial comparison between TCP and UDP.

Table 10-1   Comparison of TCP and UDP

Feature	TCP	UDP
Header size	20 bytes	8 bytes
Transmission	Not useful for time-critical data transmission	Useful for data that is only valid for a short time
Reliable		
Error checking (checksum)	Yes	Yes
Error recovery	Yes	
Ordering		

Exercise 10.1.4

Complete Table 10-1 comparing the functionality of TCP and UDP. Use your textbook and Internet research to compose your answer.

Lab 10.1 Review

1. Why is the IP address not needed at the transport layer of communication? Justify your answer.

   _____

   _____

   _____

2. For messages used for online gaming, which is a better transport protocol to use, TCP or UDP? For delivery of a web page, which is a better transport protocol to use? Justify your answer.

   _____

   _____

   _____

Lab 10.2: Common Network Ports

Approximate Lab Time: 15–20 min.

Materials Needed: Paper/Pencil, Textbook, and Internet Research

A network port is a software construct to keep incoming and outgoing traffic separate on a host machine on a shared network interface. The port to which traffic is sent does not have to be the same port number on which traffic is received, even if it is for the same application on both ends of the communication. There are a number of common port numbers that have been assigned to specific protocols for use in segregating traffic inside a host machine; you will explore these in this lab. Compile a lab report of the solutions to the assigned exercises and include a review of the work necessary to arrive at the solution.

Common Port Usage

A network port can have any number from 0 to 65535. Custom applications and configurations can make use of the higher port numbers, but most of the ports numbered below 1024 are reserved for specific applications in networking and Internet use. These ports have been identified for monitoring and use with specific applications, allowing developers a standard from which to operate and giving network administrators an ability to identify the traffic source and destination within a host by looking at the port numbers. Table 10-2 lists the most common ports and a partial list of their features and assigned uses.

Table 10-2   Table of Common Ports and Assigned Applications

Port Number	Protocol	Transport Protocol
20	File Transfer Protocol (FTP)	
21	File Transfer Protocol (FTP)	
22	Secure Shell (SSH)	
23	Telnet	
25	Simple Mail Transfer Protocol (SMTP)	
53	Domain Name System (DNS)	TCP and UDP
67	Dynamic Host Configuration Protocol (DHCP)	
69	Trivial File Transfer Protocol (TFTP)	
80	Hypertext Transfer Protocol (HTTP)	
110	Post Office Protocol version 3 (POP3)	
123	Network Time Protocol (NTP)	
143	Internet Message Access Protocol version 4 (IMAP4)	
161	Simple Network Management Protocol (SNMP)	
443	Hypertext Transfer Protocol Secure (HTTPS)	

Exercise 10.2.1

Complete Table 10-2 with the appropriate transport Layer (Layer 4) protocol (UDP or TCP) for each higher-level protocol assigned to a common port. Which transport layer protocol is most often used? Why is this true? Use your textbook and Internet research to support your answer.

_____

_____

_____

_____

Lab 10.2 Review

1. What is the benefit of assigning specific ports for certain applications and protocols (such as HTTP)? Consider port monitoring and listening in your answer. Use your textbook and Internet research to compose your answer.

_____

_____

_____

_____

_____

2. Why would an application use a custom port number for its traffic? How do custom port numbers help the software developer? How do they help a network administrator? Use your textbook and Internet research to compose your answer.

_____

_____

_____

_____

Lab 10.3: Network Management

Approximate Lab Time: 10–15 min.

Materials Needed: Paper/Pencil, Textbook, and Internet Research

Network management is an essential task for any administrator for networks ranging from small home networks to large infrastructures. Directly interfacing with network devices to test their settings and condition can be time consuming or even impossible. Fortunately, there are a number of tools to help automate this process. One of the most common in use is the Simple Network Management Protocol (SNMP), which is part of the TCP/IP protocol suite. This lab will review the structure and behavior of SNMP and how it can be a valuable tool for network monitoring. Compile a lab report of the solutions to the assigned exercises and include a review of the work necessary to arrive at the solution.

Simple Network Management Protocol

Simple Network Management Protocol (SNMP) is a useful tool for assisting a network administrator in detecting state changes and problems on devices. It uses UDP to send messages without incurring significant overhead. This also means that not all the SNMP messages will be received successfully, and any errors in the messages might not be recoverable. However, the SNMP messages only apply for a limited time, so perfect delivery is not necessary.

Exercise 10.3.1

There are three primary roles involved in SNMP: a Manager, an Agent, and a Master Agent. Briefly define each of these roles. Use your textbook or Internet research to compose your answer.

_____

_____

_____

_____

_____

Exercise 10.3.2

Two of the major classifications of messages in SNMP are Get and Set messages. What is the purpose of these messages? What happens if the action cannot be completed on a monitored host (at an Agent location)? Use your textbook or Internet research to compose your answer.

_____

_____

_____

_____

_____

_____

_____

_____

_____

_____

_____

Exercise 10.3.3

One of the most important features of SNMP is the Trap message for alerting the Manager of issues on a host machine. Give at least three events that would cause an Agent to issue a Trap message for the host it is monitoring. Why should the Manager be alerted to these events? Use your textbook or Internet research to compose your answer.

_____

_____

_____

_____

_____

_____

_____

_____

_____

_____

_____

_____

_____

Lab 10.3 Review

1. Does SNMP act as a complete solution to network monitoring? Why or why not?

_____

_____

_____

_____

_____

_____

2. A Management Information Base (MIB) is used to define the variables that are monitored and set by SNMP, allowing it to be extensible and customizable to the network and requirements of the network administrator. What are the benefits and drawbacks of this type of functionality? Use your textbook or Internet research to compose your answer.

_____

_____

_____

_____

_____

_____

Lab 10.4: Analyzing Protocols in Packet Capture

Approximate Lab Time: 25–30 min.
Prerequisite: Lab 6.3, Lab 10.2

Materials Needed: Paper/Pencil, PC Lab (Windows, OmniPeek Packet Analyzer, Internet-enabled LAN Connection, USB Wireless Adapter, Cisco Linksys Router), Textbook, and Internet Research

This final lab revisits the area of packet capturing for the purpose of exploring in greater depth the protocols in use and the traffic patterns that can be observed on a live network. Now that you have an understanding of most of the TCP/IP protocol suite, you should be able to recognize the communication paths that are created when you observe the packets being captured. For this lab, you will access various Internet services and initiate several commands over the command-line interface on your PC while recording the packets in the OmniPeek tool. You will then analyze and evaluate the results you have collected. Compile a lab report of the solutions to the assigned exercises and include a review of the work necessary to arrive at the solution.

Packet Capture Revisited

You should now have a basic understanding of how to use the OmniPeek tool for recording network traffic. For this lab, you should begin with your virtual PC connected to the Internet-enabled LAN for recording traffic to and from your machine as you attempt to connect to various resources on the Internet. You will then switch to the USB wireless adapter and connect to the wireless router to track and analyze wireless traffic.

Exercise 10.4.1

For this exercise, be sure that you have a LAN that is connected to the Internet. You will be recording the traffic generated when you connect to web resources and other local hosts. The individual units of capture you should expect for this exercise are Ethernet frames.

STEP 1. With your Internet-enabled LAN connection bridged, open the Wild Packets OmniPeek tool from the Start menu.

STEP 2. With the OmniPeek software open, click **New Capture**. This will open an options window, as shown in Figure 10-1.

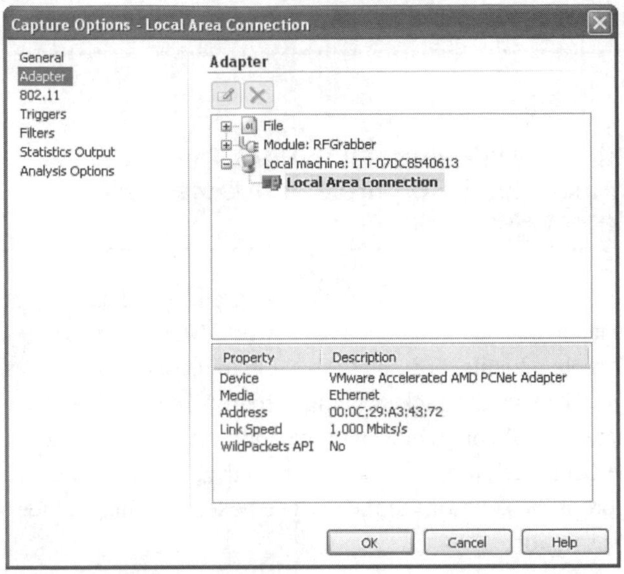

FIGURE 10-1   OmniPeek Options Window

STEP 3.   Make sure that the correct adapter is chosen (in this case the LAN connection) and click **OK**.

STEP 4.   With the capture window open, click **Start Capture**. You can see an example of the capture window in Figure 10-2.

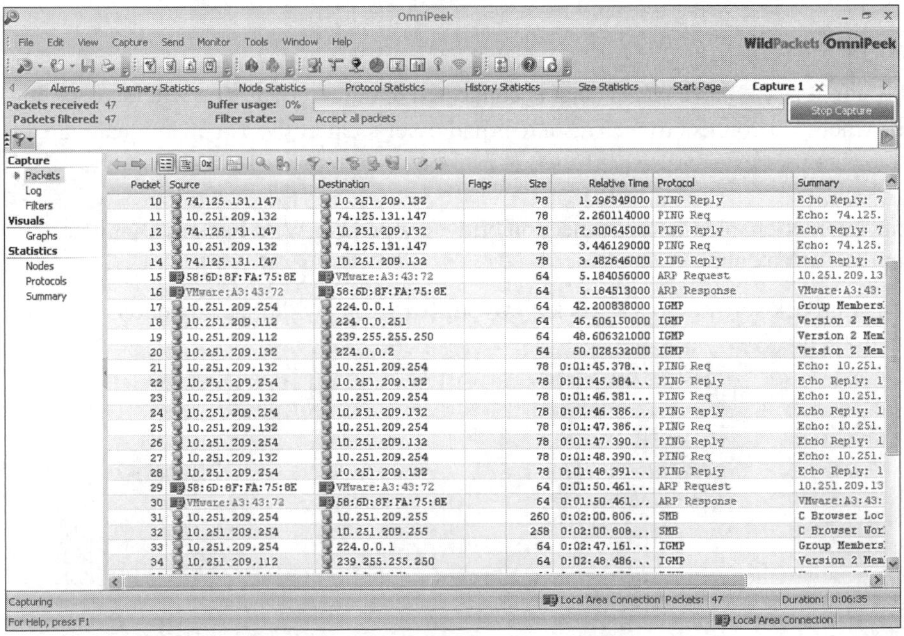

FIGURE 10-2   OmniPeek Packet Capture Window

STEP 5. Open the command-line interface. Try to ping an external Internet host (such as www.google.com). What packets appear in the capture window? What protocols are being used to complete this request? Which of these are local to the network and which of them go past the default gateway to reach an external host?

_____

_____

_____

_____

STEP 6. Use the **traceroute** command (**tracert** on Windows) for the same host you selected for the ping exercise. How do the packets differ in this communication from the packets you observed in the ping exercise?

_____

_____

_____

_____

STEP 7. Open a web browser and connect to the Internet host you selected. Observe the packets recorded for delivering the result. What packets are generated as you open the web browser itself? What is the primary protocol observed in these connections?

_____

_____

_____

_____

STEP 8. Open one of the individual HTTP packets (by double-clicking it). You can see an example of this in Figure 10-3.

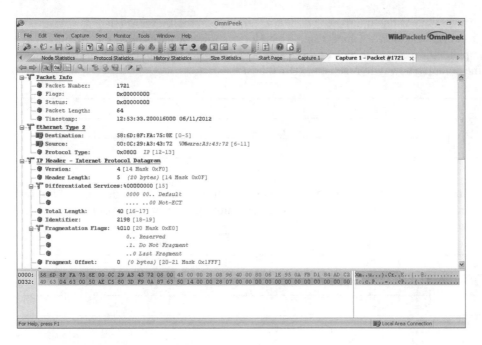

FIGURE 10-3 Captured HTTP Packet in OmniPeek

Identify the source and destination MAC address; which hosts do these represent? Identify the source and destination IP address; which hosts do these represent? Identify the source and destination ports; which transport protocol is being used?

_____

_____

_____

_____

STEP 9. Go back to the packet capture window and choose **Stop Capture**. From the left-side navigation pane, choose **Graphs** (under the heading **Visuals**). Then choose **TCP vs UDP**; choose the pie chart option from the available graphs if it is not already selected. You can see an example of this in Figure 10-4.

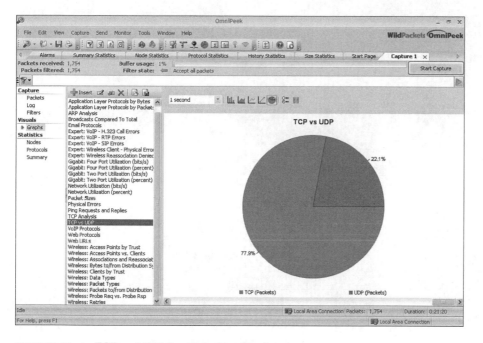

FIGURE 10-4 TCP vs UDP Graph in OmniPeek

What is the comparative use of TCP versus UDP for the packet capture you observed?

_____

STEP 10. Select the **Address Count Comparison** option from the available graphs. Switch the view to the pie chart view. What is the percentage of IP addresses used versus the percentage of physical addresses used? What is the explanation for this result?

_____

_____

_____

_____

_____

STEP 11. Select the **Nodes** item (under the heading **Statistics**) from the left-side navigation pane; you can see an example of this in Figure 10-5. Examine the destinations (the nodes).

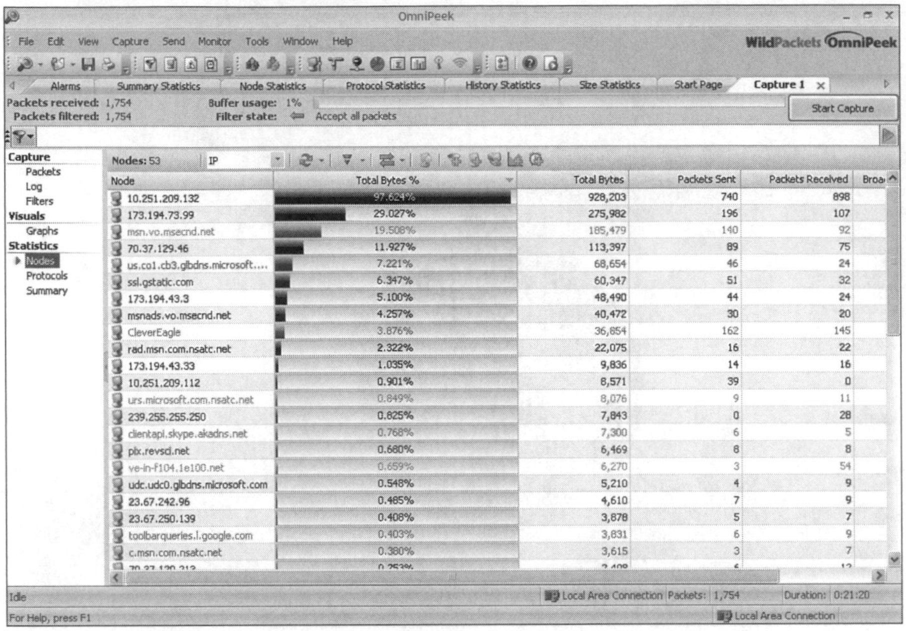

FIGURE 10-5   Nodes Statistics in OmniPeek

Which nodes reside within the local network? How much of the traffic went through the default gateway? (You can determine this by the IP address; use **ipconfig** to determine this address if you do not have it recorded.) How do you explain this percentage?

_____

_____

_____

Exercise 10.4.2

For this exercise, you should disable the LAN connection and connect the USB wireless adapter. You should then connect to the assigned AP in the room. You will be capturing the wireless transmissions from the WLAN connection for review and analysis.

> **NOTE:** Not all wireless adapters support 802.11 packet capture. Most will allow you to capture the traffic as Ethernet frames instead of wireless packets.

If you do not have OmniPeek open already, you should open it before you begin. Choose **New Capture** and select the wireless adapter for packet capture. Connect to the AP and select **Start Capture** in OmniPeek. What differences do you see from the wireless traffic compared to the LAN traffic?

_____

_____

_____

_____

_____

_____

Lab 10.4 Review

1. What tools you have used in the lab have been the most helpful in identifying and explaining network concepts? Have the labs improved your confidence in your own understanding of networking technology and how devices communicate?

_____

_____

_____

_____

_____

_____

2. In what areas of the network do you still need to get a better understanding? What is your plan for exploring these topics in more detail?

_____

_____

_____

_____

_____

_____